W9-BGO-360

Through the BIBLE Puzzles

for Kids 8-12

STANDARD PUBLISHING ™

Cincinnati, Ohio

Through the Bible Puzzles

Standard Publishing, Cincinnati, Ohio
A division of Standex International Corporation
©1994, 2001 by Standard Publishing
All rights reserved
Printed in the United States of America
Previously published under the title *Through the Bible in a Year Puzzles*

07   06   05   04   03   02   9   8   7   6   5   4   3   2

Edited by Henrietta Gambill
Revised by Theresa Hayes
Cover design by Jeff Jansen

All scripture quotations, unless otherwise indicated, are taken from the HOLY BIBLE, NEW INTERNATIONAL VERSION®. NIV®. Copyright ©1973, 1978, 1984 by International Bible Society. Used by permission of Zondervan Publishing House. All rights reserved.

Scripture marked ICB quoted from the *International Children's Bible, New Century Version,* copyright ©1986, 1988 by Word Publishing, Dallas, Texas 75039. Used by permission.

ISBN 0-7847-1171-2

Table of Contents

Let There Be . . .

Read Genesis 1:1-25. Starting with Day 1, find the correct path through the maze to the things that God created on that day. Do this until you have matched all the days with the correct pictures.

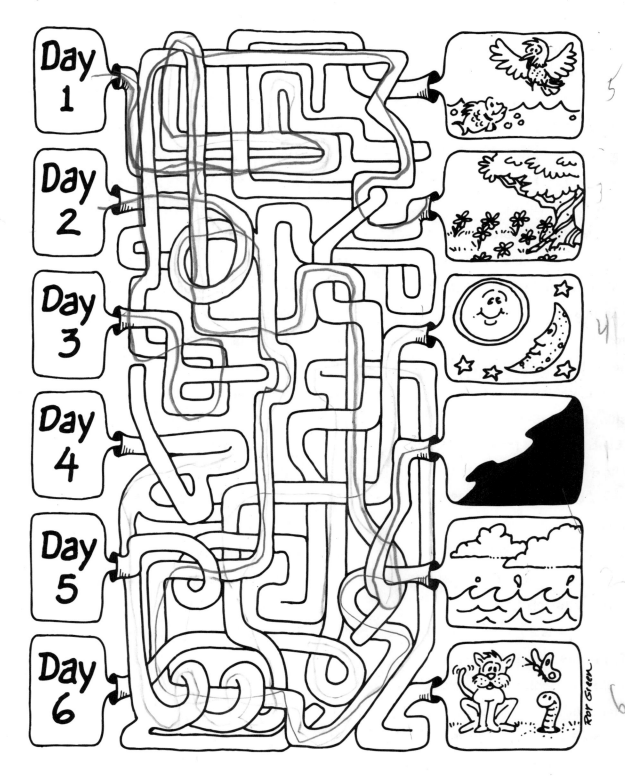

 Through the Bible Puzzles, © 2001 by Standard Publishing • Permission granted to photocopy for classroom use only.

The Beginning

Do you know how the world began? Use the graph to find out. Each column has a number and each row has a letter. Use the number and the letter combination to solve this puzzle. (Example 5C = G.) Read how God did this in Genesis 1:1–2:3.

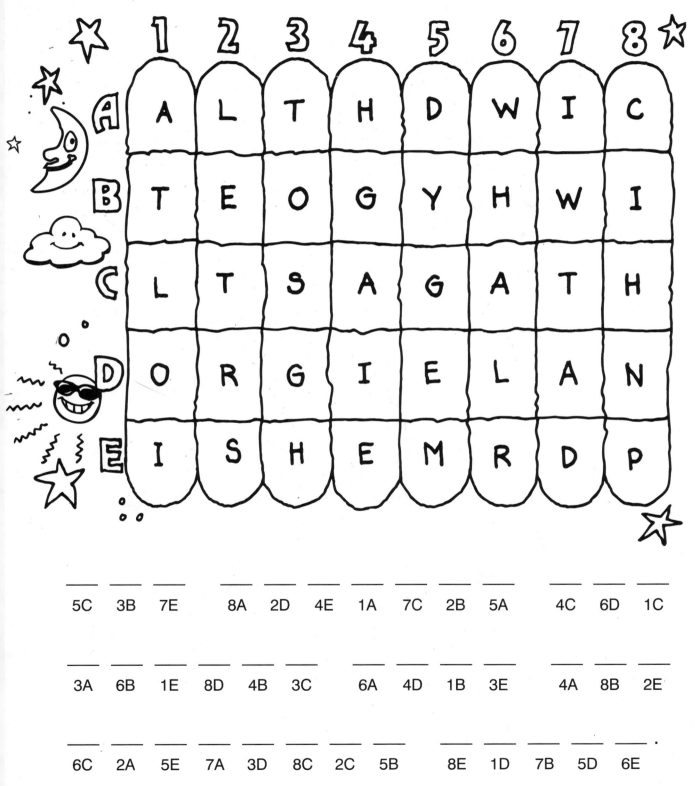

	1	2	3	4	5	6	7	8
A	A	L	T	H	D	W	I	C
B	T	E	O	G	Y	H	W	I
C	L	T	S	A	G	A	T	H
D	O	R	G	I	E	L	A	N
E	I	S	H	E	M	R	D	P

___ ___ ___   ___ ___ ___ ___ ___ ___ ___   ___ ___ ___
5C 3B 7E   8A 2D 4E 1A 7C 2B 5A   4C 6D 1C

___ ___ ___ ___ ___ ___   ___ ___ ___ ___   ___ ___ ___
3A 6B 1E 8D 4B 3C   6A 4D 1B 3E   4A 8B 2E

___ ___ ___ ___ ___ ___ ___ ___   ___ ___ ___ ___ ___ .
6C 2A 5E 7A 3D 8C 2C 5B   8E 1D 7B 5D 6E

Through the Bible Puzzles, © 2001 by Standard Publishing • Permission granted to photocopy for classroom use only.

Something Special

Beginning with column #1, go down each column until you come to a dot. Copy the letter that is found to the left of the dot onto the first blank below. Some columns will have more than one letter. Put a piece of paper on the right-hand side of the puzzle. Move it to reveal one column at a time. When completed, you will find out about God's special creation. Read Genesis 1:27.

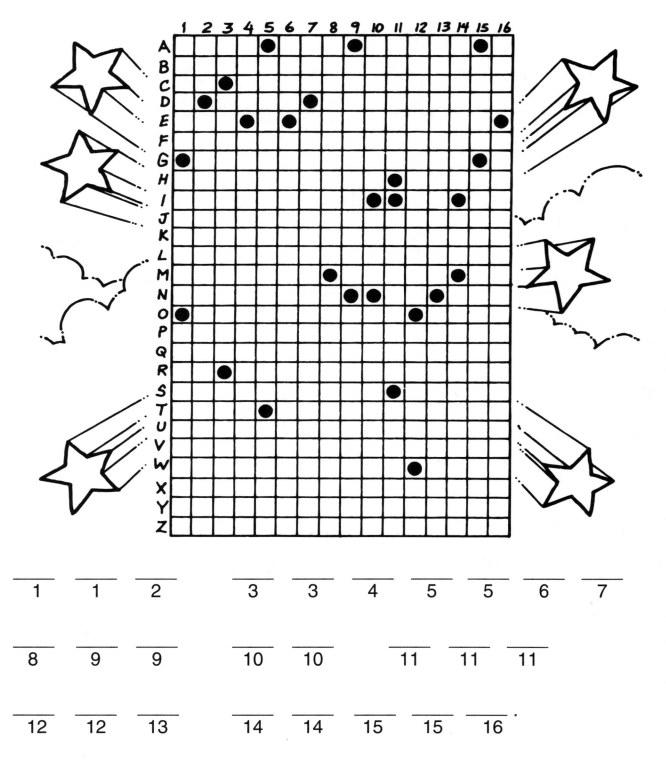

—— —— —— ——— ——— —— —— ———
 1   1   2   3   3   4   5   5   6   7

—— —— —— ——— ——— ——— ——— ———
 8   9   9   10   10   11 11 11

—— —— —— ——— ——— ——— ——— ———·
12 12 13   14   14   15   15   16

Through the Bible Puzzles, © 2001 by Standard Publishing • Permission granted to photocopy for classroom use only.

Strange Tree

A sad event occurred at this tree to make it different from all other trees. Use the code from the strange tree to solve the puzzle. Read the story in Genesis 2:15-17; 3:1-23.

Where Are You?

Starting with Row #1, move the letter directly below the number 1 to the second puzzle box marked #1. Move all the letters in each column to the empty boxes before you move on to the next number. Cross out each letter after you move it. When completed, read the question in the second puzzle box. Then answer the question on the blank lines below. Read Genesis 3:8-19.

1	2	3	4	5	6	7	8	9	10	11	12	13	14
H	I	D	H	Y	F	D	I	T	R	Y	D	T	M
A	N	W	E	E	V	E	O	M		G	O	A	O
		D				R		D		A		D	?

1	2	3	4	5	6	7	8	9	10	11	12	13	14
	W	H	Y			D	I	D		A	D	A	M
A	N	d		e	V	E		T	r	y		T	B
H	i	D	e		F	r	O	M		G	O	d	?

_____

_____

Through the Bible Puzzles, © 2001 by Standard Publishing • Permission granted to photocopy for classroom use only.

Offerings

To solve this puzzle, find all the letters in each shape. Unscramble the letters found in the same shape to discover why God looked with favor on Abel's offering and not with favor on Cain's offering. Then read the story in Genesis 4:1-15.

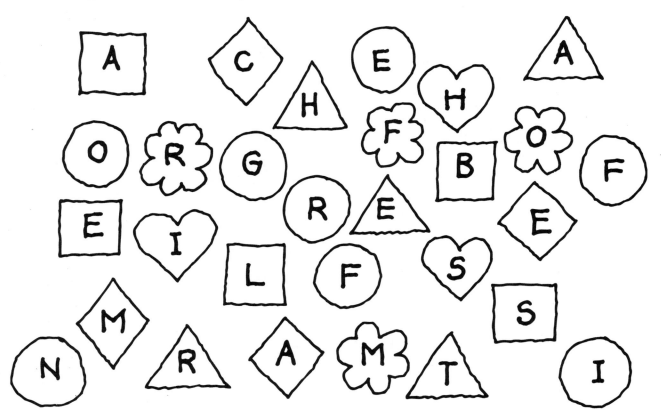

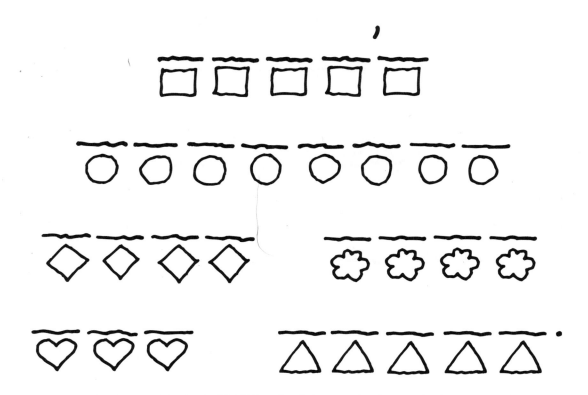

Rainbows

God put the rainbow in the sky as a sign of the covenant he made with all people. Use the code to discover the covenant God made with us. Read about the promise in Genesis 9:8-15.

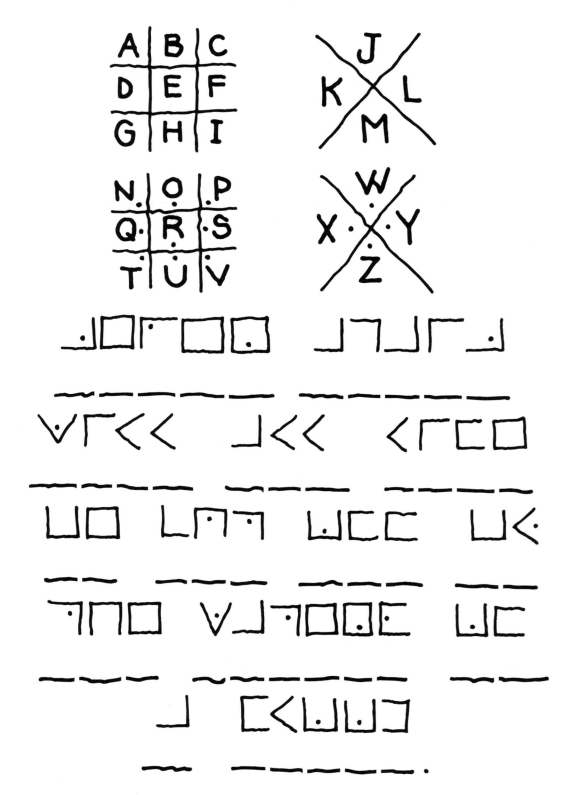

 Through the Bible Puzzles, © 2001 by Standard Publishing • Permission granted to photocopy for classroom use only.

The Promise

Abram was told to go to a new land. Complete the math problems and decode the promise God gave to Abram. Check your work in Genesis 12:2. Read about Abram's journey in Genesis 12:1-7.

A = 1 • B = 2 • C = 3 • D = 4 • E = 5 • F = 6 • G = 7 • H = 8 • I = 9 • J = 10
K = 11 • L = 12 • M = 13 • N = 14 • O = 15 • P = 16 • Q = 17 • R = 18 • S = 19
T = 20 •U = 21 • V = 22 • W = 23 • X = 24 • Y = 25 • Z = 26

| ___ | ___ | ___ | ___ | ___ |
| 5 + 4 | 12 + 11 | 6 + 3 | 4 x 3 | 8 + 4 |

| ___ | ___ | ___ | ___ | ___ | ___ | ___ |
| 6 + 7 | 8 − 7 | 6 + 5 | 3 + 2 | 5 x 5 | 5 x 3 | 14 + 7 |

| ___ | ___ | ___ | ___ | ___ |
| 7 + 2 | 7 + 7 | 5 x 4 | 8 + 7 | 5 − 4 |

| ___ | ___ | ___ | ___ | ___ |
| 4 + 3 | 6 x 3 | 4 + 1 | 1 + 0 | 10 + 10 |

| ___ | ___ | ___ | ___ | ___ | ___ |
| 7 x 2 | 9 − 8 | 10 x 2 | 8 + 1 | 6 + 9 | 9 + 5 |

| ___ | ___ | ___ | ___ |
| 3 − 2 | 6 + 8 | 2 + 2 | 3 x 3 |

| ___ | ___ | ___ | ___ |
| 16 + 7 | 12 − 3 | 6 x 2 | 7 + 5 |

| ___ | ___ | ___ | ___ | ___ |
| 1 + 1 | 9 + 3 | 9 − 4 | 12 + 7 | 4 + 15 |

| ___ | ___ | ___ |
| 15 + 10 | 11 + 4 | 7 x 3 |

Through the Bible Puzzles, © 2001 by Standard Publishing • Permission granted to photocopy for classroom use only.

Separation

Abram and his nephew Lot agreed to separate because there was not enough grass on the land to feed all of their flocks. Follow the directions carefully for a wonderful example of unselfish love shown by Abram. Read the story in Genesis 13:1-9.

1. Change the letter **O** to **T**. 2. Change the letter **E** to **G**. 3. Change the letter **H** to **I**.
4. Change the letter **T** to **O**. 5. Change the letter **G** to **E**. 6. Change the letter **I** to **H**.
7. Keep the other letters **the same**.

H F   Y T U   E T   O T   O I G   L G F O,

‗ ‗   ‗ ‗ ‗   ‗ ‗   ‗ ‗   ‗ ‗ ‗   ‗ ‗ ‗ ‗,

H' L L   E T   O T   O I G   R H E I O;   H F

‗ ‗ ‗   ‗ ‗   ‗ ‗   ‗ ‗ ‗   ‗ ‗ ‗ ‗ ‗;   ‗ ‗

Y T U   E T   O T   O I G R H E I O,   H' L L

‗ ‗ ‗   ‗ ‗   ‗ ‗   ‗ ‗ ‗ ‗ ‗ ‗ ‗,   ‗ ‗ ‗

E T   O T   O I G   L G F O.

‗ ‗   ‗ ‗   ‗ ‗ ‗   ‗ ‗ ‗ ‗.

   Through the Bible Puzzles, © 2001 by Standard Publishing • Permission granted to photocopy for classroom use only.

Who's Who?

Read Genesis 18:1-14. Use the clues below to fill in the answer boxes on the right. If some of the letters appear in the next answer, the arrows will show you where to place them.

1. Man near the great trees of Mamre (v. 1).

2. The visitors (v. 2).

3. The visitors asked about whom (v. 9)?

4. The one who prepared the meal (v. 7).

5. The visitor who spoke (v. 10).

6. "Will I really have a ____ now that I am old?" (v. 13).

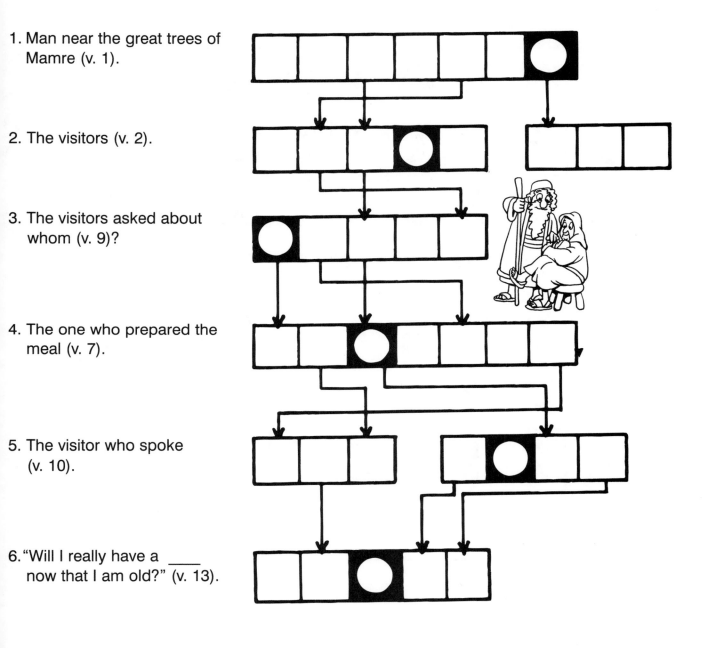

Unscramble the circled letters to solve the puzzle below. The three visitors came to give Abraham and Sarah a

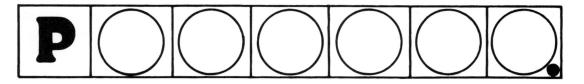

P ◯ ◯ ◯ ◯ ◯ ◯.

Through the Bible Puzzles, © 2001 by Standard Publishing • Permission granted to photocopy for classroom use only.

A Lot to Learn

Fill in the missing words in each sentence below from Genesis 19. Place an X through the letters that spell the missing words in each line of the box below.

Then write the remaining letters from left to right, line by line, in the blanks at the bottom. These letters will spell out an important lesson from Genesis 19.

1.	S	S	O	I	D	N	O	M
2.	B	R	L	I	N	O	T	G
3.	D	E	S	S	T	R	O	Y
4.	P	W	I	U	F	N	E	I
5.	S	U	S	L	F	U	H	R
6.	M	P	I	L	E	L	A	R
7.	R	I	N	S	T	I	N	G

1. The two angels arrived at _____ (v. 1).

2. The angels spoke to _____ (v. 12).

3. They told him the Lord was about to _____ the city (v. 14).

4. They told him to flee with his _____ and daughters to the mountains (v. 16, 17).

5. Then the Lord rained down burning _____ on Sodom and Gomorrah (v. 24).

6. But Lot's wife looked back and became a _____ of salt (v. 26).

7. The next morning Abraham looked toward Sodom and Gomorrah and saw dense smoke _____ from the land (v. 28).

___ ___ ___ ___   ___ ___ ___   ___ ___ ___ ___ ___ ___ ___

 Through the Bible Puzzles, © 2001 by Standard Publishing • Permission granted to photocopy for classroom use only.

Stop!

Abraham was going to follow God's command and offer his son, Isaac, as a burnt offering. Write the letter that comes after the letter given to see what an angel of the Lord said to Abraham. Read the story in Genesis 22:1-13.

"C N   M N S   K Z X   Z   G Z M C   N M

— —   — — —   — — —   —   — — — —   — —

S G D   A N X,"   G D   R Z H C.   "C N   M N S

— — —   — — —   — —   — — — —   — —   — — —

C N   Z M X S G H M F   S N   G H L.   M N V   H

— —   — — — — — — —   — —   — — —   — — —   —

J M N V   S G Z S   X N T   E D Z Q   F N C,

— — — —   — — — —   — — —   — — — —   — — —

A D B Z T R D   X N T   G Z U D   M N S

— — — — — — —   — — —   — — — —   — — —

V H S G G D K C   E Q N L   L D   X N T Q   R N M,

— — — — — — — —   — — — —   — —   — — — —   — — —

X N T Q   N M K X   R N M."

— — — —   — — — —   — — —

Family Ties

Abraham's servant was sent to find a wife for Isaac. He found Rebekah, the granddaughter of Abraham's brother. Bethuel, Rebekah's father, told the servant to take Rebekah so that she could be the wife of his master's son. The last part of each word is at the top of the page. Finish each word with its correct ending to discover why Bethuel agreed to send his daughter to a strange land. Read the story in Genesis 24:32-52.

HE __ __ I__ REBE__ __ __; TA__ __

H__ __ A__ __ G__, AN__ L__ __

HE__ BE__ __ __ __ __ T__ __ WI__ __

O__ YO__ __ MAS__ __ __'__ S__ __,

A__ TH__ LO__ __ H__ __

DIR__ __ __ __ __.

 Through the Bible Puzzles, © 2001 by Standard Publishing • Permission granted to photocopy for classroom use only.

Brothers

Jacob and Esau were twin sons of Isaac. One of the twins did a very foolish thing. Discover what happened by coloring in each box where the answer does not equal 24. Then read about Jacob and Esau in Genesis 25:27-34 and Genesis 27:1-44.

84-27= A	14+10= E	24X0= O	8X3= S	41-28= R	28-4= A	4X6= U	9+9= T
12+12= S	17+7= O	20+14= A	2X12= L	47-24= E	23+14= R	6+18= D	37-8= E
3X12= B	42-22= E	51-27= H	35-11= I	64-20= H	19+5= S	9+17= T	24X1= B
4+20= I	8X6= A	55-31= R	14+10= T	81-55= O	72÷3= H	7X4= A	11+16= E
18-6= S	9+15= R	49-24= G	9x4= O	48-24= I	14+13= D	3+21= G	68-3= R
37-13= H	2+22= T	6X7= I	38-4= H	48÷2= T	7+8= T	16+8= O	68-44= J
22+22= O	30-6= A	16+7= M	24x1= C	30-5= L	25-1= O	23+1= B	3x6= Z

Through the Bible Puzzles, © 2001 by Standard Publishing • Permission granted to photocopy for classroom use only.

Heavenly Ladder

Jacob dreamed he saw angels ascending and descending on a stairway to Heaven. Decode the puzzle to discover why Jacob called the place "Bethel" after he awoke. Then read Genesis 28:10-22.

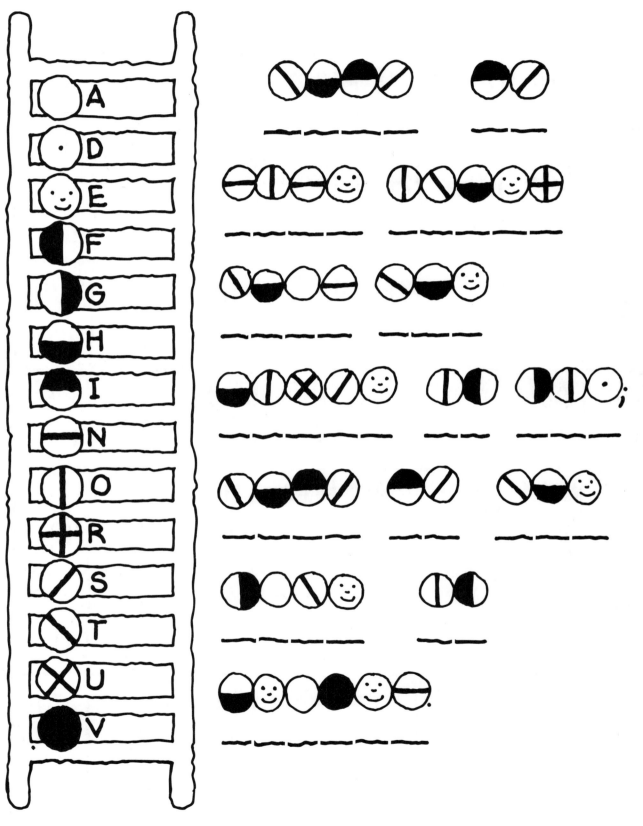

Through the Bible Puzzles, © 2001 by Standard Publishing • Permission granted to photocopy for classroom use only.

Children of Israel

The twelve sons of Israel became the twelve tribes of Israel. Their names are listed below. All the boxes connect with a box containing the same letter. After you find the names of the twelve sons of Israel, check your work in Genesis 35:23-26.

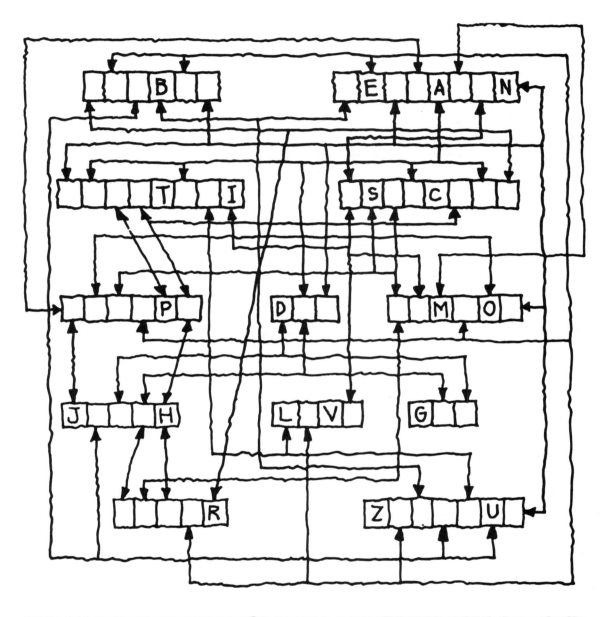

Oh Brother!

Read about Joseph in Genesis 37:3-36. Then use the clues to unscramble the words. Write the circled letters in order in the spaces at the bottom of the page.

Verse 3. _____ loved Joseph more than any of his sons.

SEARIL __ __ __ (○) __ __

Verse 5. Joseph had a _____ .

MRDAE __ __ __ __ (○)

Verse 12. Joseph's brothers had gone to graze their _____ .

COLFSK __ __ __ __ __ __

Verses 21, 22. This brother tried to rescue Joseph.

BUERNE __ (○) __ __ __ __

Verse 23. Joseph was wearing a richly ornamented _____ .

BEOR (○) __ __ __

Verse 24. Joseph's brothers threw him into a _____ .

NERTISC __ __ __ __ __ (○) __

Verse 28. His brothers sold him to _____ merchants.

NATIIMEDI __ __ (○) __ __ __ __ __ __

Verse 36. The Midianites sold Joseph in _____ .

TGEPY (○) __ __ __ __

Unscramble the circled letters to fill in the blanks below.

Verse 19. Joseph's brothers called him a ____ ____ ____ ____ ____ ____ ____ .

 Through the Bible Puzzles, © 2001 by Standard Publishing • Permission granted to photocopy for classroom use only.

Who's in Charge?

Read Genesis 41:15-57 about Joseph in Egypt. Then use the code to solve the puzzle. Find the letter in the message on the outside circle. Match it with the letter across from it on the inside circle.

Z R K B K Y R   C K S N   D Y   T Y C O Z R,   "C S X M O   Q Y N

R K C   W K N O   K V V   D R S C   U X Y G X   D Y   I Y E, . . .

S   R O B O L I   Z E D   I Y E   S X   M R K B Q O

Y P   D R O   G R Y V O   V K X N   Y P   O Q I Z D."

Through the Bible Puzzles, © 2001 by Standard Publishing • Permission granted to photocopy for classroom use only.

Food for Thought

Read Genesis 41:38-43, 46-49, 53-57. Then write the food names from each square in the matching line of the acrostic puzzle. When complete, the shaded area will tell about the crisis Joseph warned Pharaoh was coming.

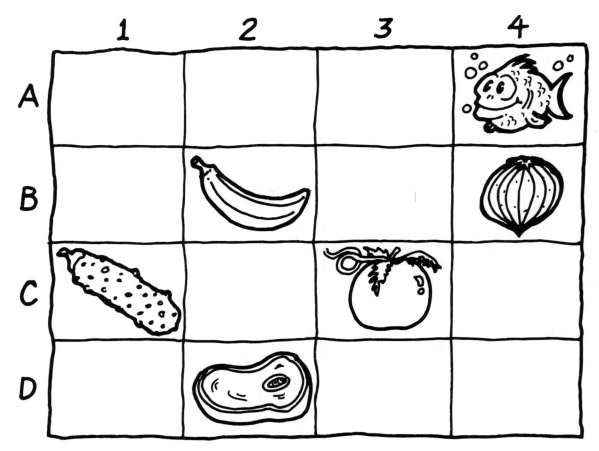

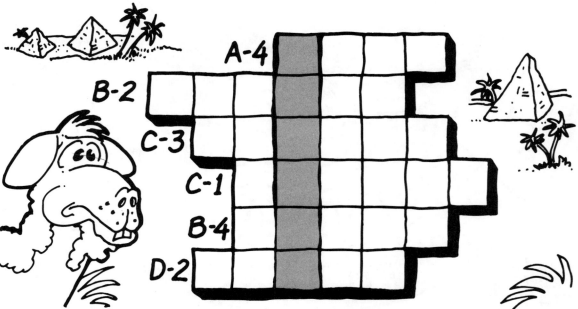

A-4

B-2

C-3

C-1

B-4

D-2

   Through the Bible Puzzles, © 2001 by Standard Publishing • Permission granted to photocopy for classroom use only.

Family Reunion

Read about Joseph's reunion with his family in Genesis 42, 45, and 47. Then mark an 0 over the statements that are true and an X over the false ones. If you're correct, you will have three X's or O's in a row.

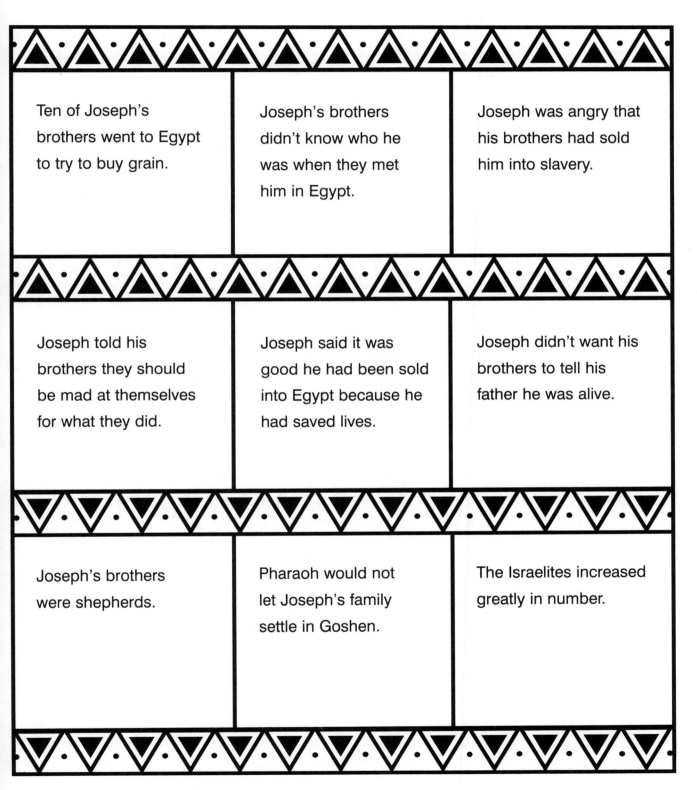

Ten of Joseph's brothers went to Egypt to try to buy grain.

Joseph's brothers didn't know who he was when they met him in Egypt.

Joseph was angry that his brothers had sold him into slavery.

Joseph told his brothers they should be mad at themselves for what they did.

Joseph said it was good he had been sold into Egypt because he had saved lives.

Joseph didn't want his brothers to tell his father he was alive.

Joseph's brothers were shepherds.

Pharaoh would not let Joseph's family settle in Goshen.

The Israelites increased greatly in number.

Through the Bible Puzzles, © 2001 by Standard Publishing • Permission granted to photocopy for classroom use only.

Egyptian Inscription

Read Exodus 1:1-5. These verses tell the names of the twelve sons of Israel. These men and their families moved to the land of Egypt to escape the famine. The names of these twelve men are hidden in the Egyptian inscriptions below. Can you find them?

Through the Bible Puzzles, © 2001 by Standard Publishing • Permission granted to photocopy for classroom use only.

Baby in a Basket

Read Exodus 2:1-10 about an important child. To solve the puzzle, first work the math problems. Then, beginning with the square that contains the answer 1, write the words in order on the lines below.

4+4	23-10	11+8	43-22	100-99	14-2	36-32
him	he	him	saying	when	and	grew
5+6	12+12	25-20	13+15	100-80	100-94	9+7
daughter	him	older	water	Moses	she	son
20-3	92-90	20+5	28-14	18+9	11+11	7+2
She	the	out	became	the	I	to
30-20	12+6	8-1	21+2	18+8	5-2	8+7
Pharaoh's	named	took	drew	of	child	her

_____

_____

_____

Scrambled Plagues

One of the ten plagues God sent to the Egyptians was frogs. Unscramble the words on the frogs to discover eight other plagues God sent. If you need help, read Exodus 7–10.

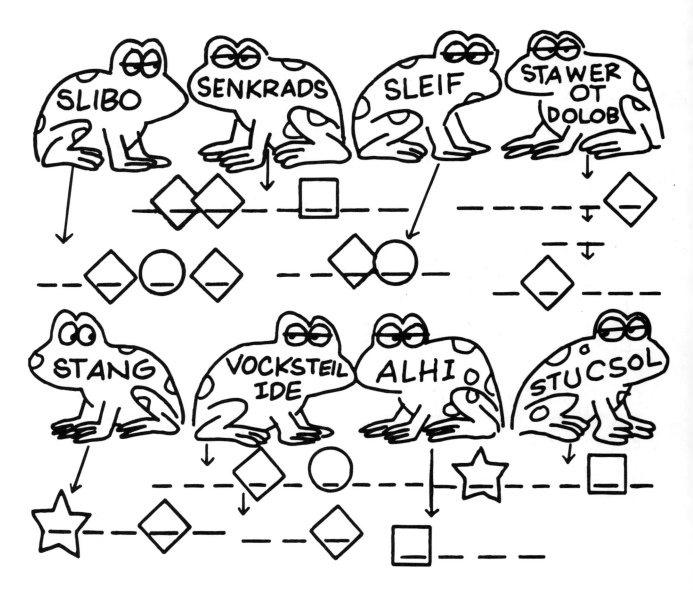

Now put each circled letter in a circle below, each letter with a square around it in a square below, and so on. Unscramble the letters to find God's message to Pharaoh.

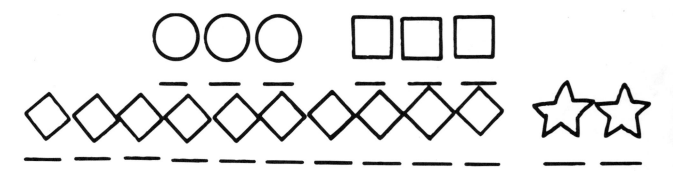

 Through the Bible Puzzles, © 2001 by Standard Publishing • Permission granted to photocopy for classroom use only.

Eat and Run

Read about God's plan to free Israel in Exodus 12:3, 7, 8, 11-14. Then connect the dots in order from 1-73 to find the Bible name for this event.

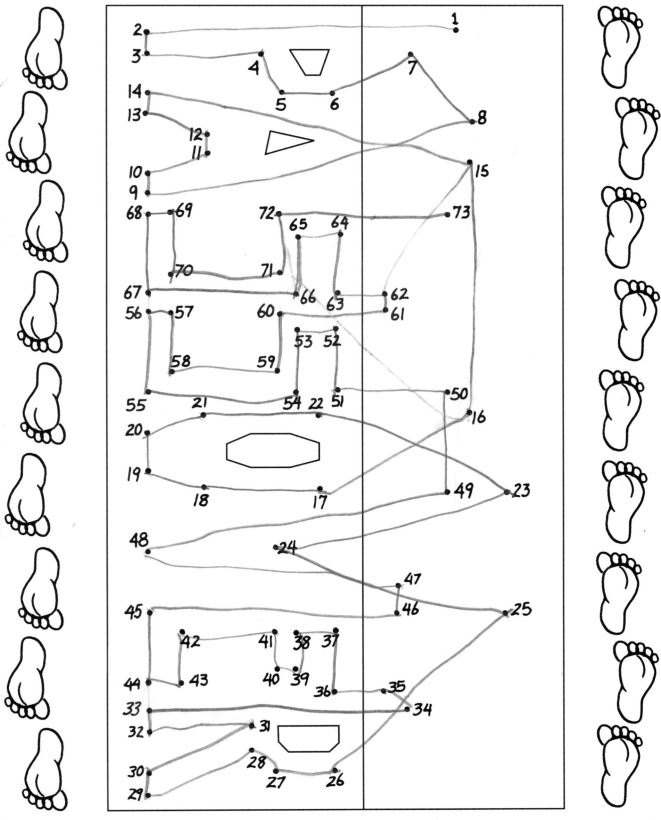

Our Passover Lamb

Read Exodus 12:21-31 to answer each question. If the answer is true, circle the letter under T. If it is false, circle the letter under F. Write the circled letters on the correct blanks below. Then read 1 Corinthians 5:7.

	T	F
1. Moses told the Israelites to put blood on the top and side of their doorframes.	H	R
2. The blood was from goats.	J	U
3. The firstborn in every family without blood on its doorframe would die.	S	M
4. The firstborn animals would die.	J	L
5. Moses told them all to stay in their homes until morning.	I	A
6. The Lord struck down the firstborn Egyptians at 2:00 in the morning.	W	C
7. Pharaoh's oldest child was killed.	E	I
8. The oldest child of every prisoner in the dungeons was killed.	T	R
9. The Lord "passed over" the homes that had blood on the doorframes.	S	D
10. The Jews remember the event by celebrating Passover.	S	U
11. While it was still night Pharaoh told Moses to take the Israelites out of Egypt.	R	E

‾‾ ‾‾ ‾‾ ‾‾ ‾‾   ‾‾ ‾‾ ‾‾ ‾‾ ‾‾ ‾‾
4 7 3 2 9   6 1 11 5 10 8

Through the Bible Puzzles, © 2001 by Standard Publishing • Permission granted to photocopy for classroom use only.

Walls of Water

Find out what happened in Exodus 14:15-31 by going through the maze. Pick up the letters as you go and write them on the lines below.

_____

_____

Food for Thought

In your mind, match the puzzle pieces. Write each word in the matching puzzle piece to complete the verse.

then   filled   twilight

Know   eat

bread   morning   meat

God   Lord

At [_____] you will [_____]

[_____] and in the [_____] you will

be [_____] with [_____]. [_____]

you will [_____] that I am the

[_____] your [_____]. Exodus 16:12

 Through the Bible Puzzles, © 2001 by Standard Publishing • Permission granted to photocopy for classroom use only.

The Ten Commandments

Use the code to find the missing word in each of the Ten Commandments. Then read about the Commandments in Exodus 20:1-17.

1. You shall have no other ____ before me.
   O 8 X *

2. You shall not make or worship _____.
   L X 8 > *

3. You shall not misuse God's _____.
   V • ∧ ⊠

4. Remember the _____ day by keeping it holy.
   * • ∕ ∕ • 8 □

5. _____ your father and mother.
   □ 8 V 8 +

6. You shall not _____.
   ∧ ∞ + X ⊠ +

7. You shall not commit _____.
   • X ∞ > 8 ⊠ + ⊞

8. You shall not _____.
   * 8 ⊠ • >

9. You shall not give _____ testimony.
   ■ • > * ⊠

10. You shall not _____.
    ∖ 8 > ⊠ 8

Through the Bible Puzzles, © 2001 by Standard Publishing • Permission granted to photocopy for classroom use only.

Beware of Imitations

Is it possible to have a substitute for God? Color in each box where the answer does not equal 24 to see what God says in Exodus 20:3.

9 x 4 =	14 + 10 =	14 + 13 =	8 x 3 =	68 – 30 =	6 x 7 =	28 – 4 =
T	Y	H	O	E	E	U
35 – 11=	18 – 16 =	19 + 5 =	48 ÷ 2 =	49 – 24 =	16 + 8 =	68 – 44 =
S	O	H	A	N	L	L
11 + 16 =	24 x 1 =	7 x 4 =	4 + 20 =	55 – 31 =	81 – 55 =	14 + 10 =
A	H	U	A	V	N	E
3 x 12 =	42 – 22 =	72 ÷ 3 =	64 – 20 =	9 + 17 =	9 + 15 =	8 x 6 =
O	R	N	R	Y	O	U
48 – 24 =	24 x 1 =	21 + 5 =	63 – 39 =	11 + 13 =	37 – 8 =	97 – 73 =
O	T	E	H	E	W	R
51 – 27 =	47 – 24 =	3 + 21 =	23 + 14 =	99 – 75 =	52 – 27 =	83 – 59 =
G	A	O	F	D	O	S
4 x 6 =	12 + 12 =	17 + 7 =	9 + 9 =	36 – 12 =	2 x 12 =	6 + 18 =
B	E	F	A	O	R	E
24 x 0 =	41 – 28 =	37 – 13 =	12 x 12 =	84 – 27 =	2 + 22 =	20 + 14 =
A	R	M	H	A	E	N

 Through the Bible Puzzles, © 2001 by Standard Publishing • Permission granted to photocopy for classroom use only.

Respect

Match the words in the shapes with the same shapes in the tablet. Read the rest of Exodus 20:7 to find out more about God's name. Check James 3:2-5, 7-10, and Ephesians 4:29 for more about our words.

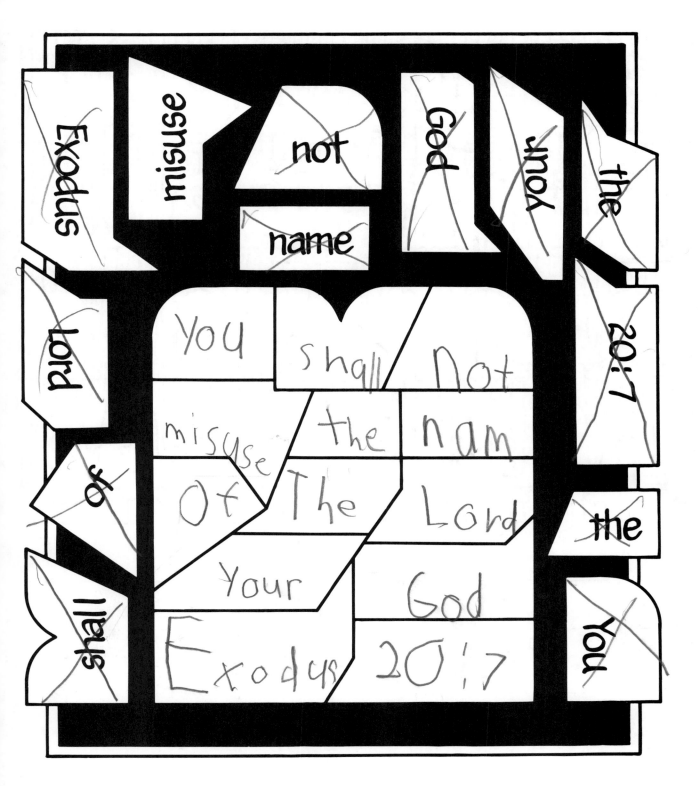

Through the Bible Puzzles, © 2001 by Standard Publishing • Permission granted to photocopy for classroom use only.

Ring the Bells

Collect all the letters with the number 1 to spell the first word below. Do the same with numbers 2 through 8. After collecting all the letters in the proper order, you will know what to do on this special day. Read Exodus 20:8.

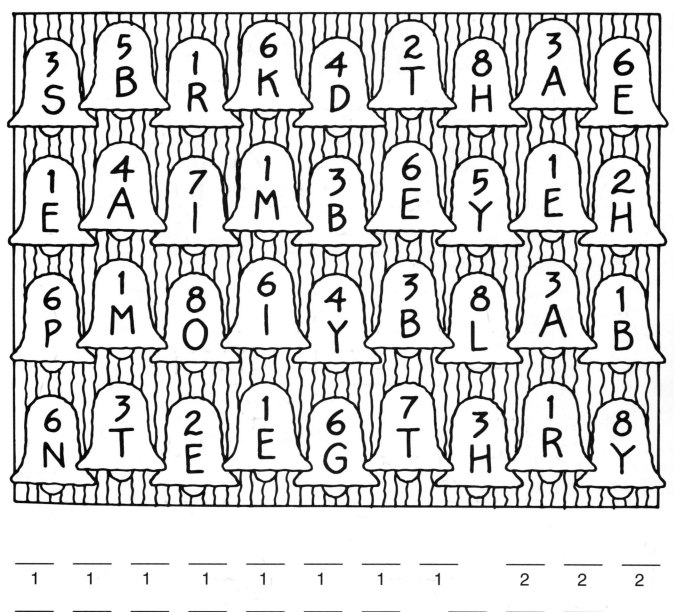

___ ___ ___ ___ ___ ___ ___ ___   ___ ___ ___
1   1   1   1   1   1   1   1   2   2   2

___ ___ ___ ___ ___ ___ ___   ___ ___ ___
3   3   3   3   3   3   3   4   4   4

___ ___   ___ ___ ___ ___ ___ ___ ___
5   5   6   6   6   6   6   6   6

___ ___   ___ ___ ___ ___ .
7   7   8   8   8   8

Through the Bible Puzzles, © 2001 by Standard Publishing • Permission granted to photocopy for classroom use only.

The Promise

Complete the puzzle below to read the first commandment with a promise. All the boxes connect with a box containing the same letter. After you finish the puzzle, check your work in Exodus 20:12.

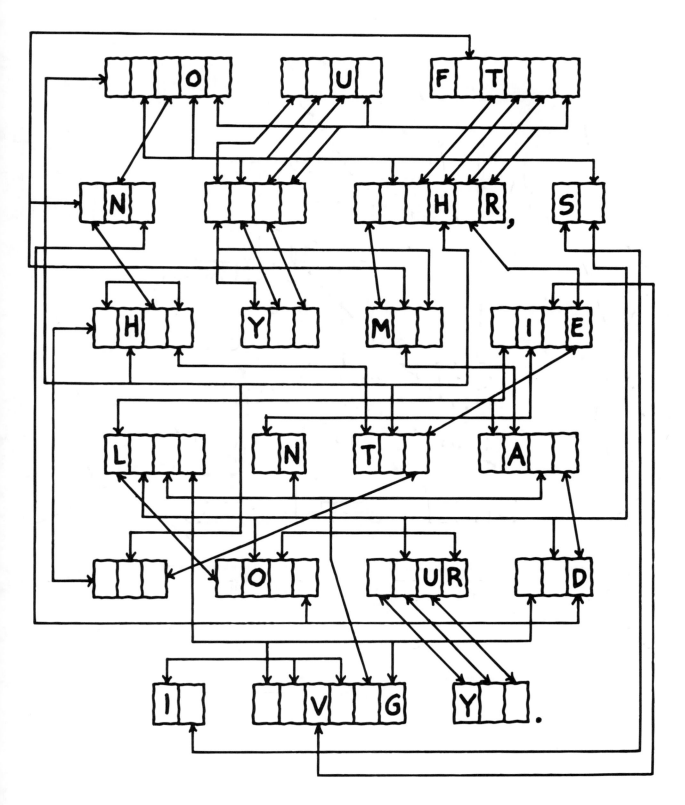

Honesty

Find Exodus 20:16 by going through the maze. Pick up the letters as you go and put them on the lines below. There is only one correct path.

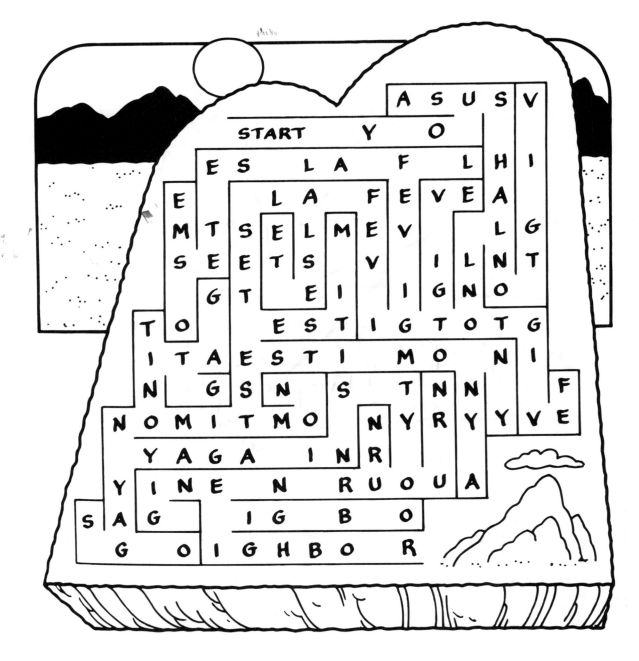

_____

_____

_____ .

Through the Bible Puzzles, © 2001 by Standard Publishing • Permission granted to photocopy for classroom use only.

Leave It Alone

Use the secret code to discover how we should behave toward our neighbor. Find each letter in the message below on the inside circle. Match it with the letter across from it on the outside circle, and put those letters on the boxes below. Read Exodus 20:17.

☐☐☐   ☐☐☐☐☐   ☐☐☐   ☐☐☐☐☐   ☐☐☐☐
O E K   I X Q B B   D E J   S E L U J   O E K H

☐☐☐☐☐☐☐☐   ☐☐☐☐
D U Y W X R E H' I   X E K I U.

☐☐☐   ☐☐☐☐☐   ☐☐☐   ☐☐☐☐☐
O E K   I X Q B B   D E J   S E L U J

☐☐☐☐☐☐☐   ☐☐☐☐   ☐☐☐☐☐☐   ☐☐
Q D O J X Y D W   J X Q J   R U B E D W I   J E

☐☐☐☐   ☐☐☐☐☐☐☐
O E K H   D U Y W X R E H.

The Tabernacle

Read Exodus 25:1-9. Then fill in the boxes to find God's promise. Each box that connects to another box contains the same letter.

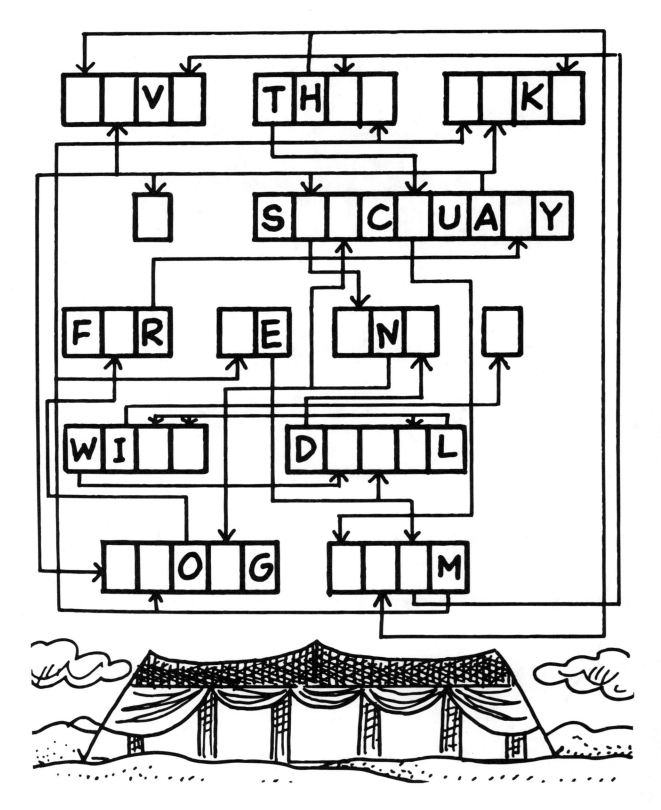

Written in Stone

Find the shape on the outside of the puzzle that matches a shape in the tablet. Write the word from that shape on the matching shape. Read Exodus 32:1-6, 15-20.

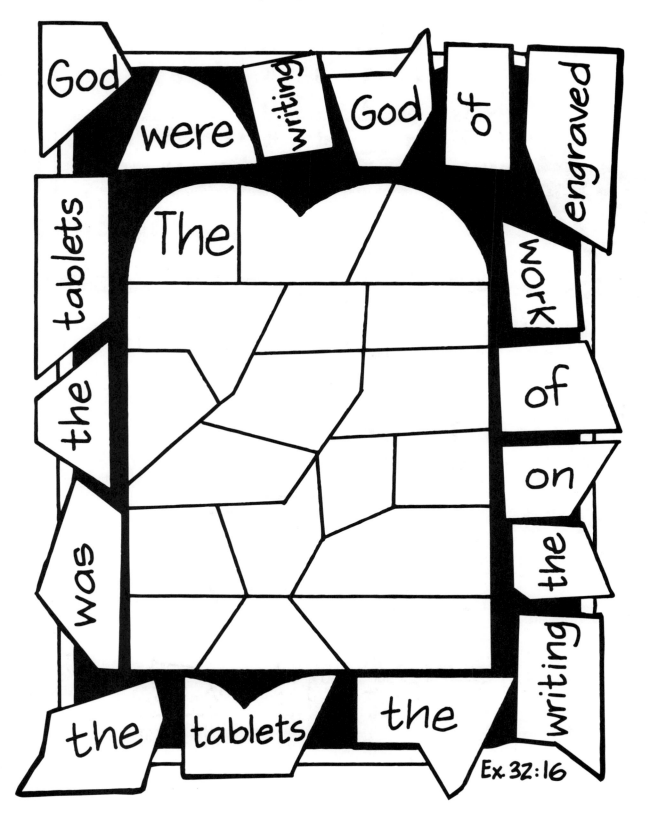

In Numbers

Below each blank are two numbers. The first number names a ROW (1–3) in the code key. The second number names a COLUMN (1–7) in the code key. For example, 13 means look in row 1 and column 3 for the letter. Read the Bible story in Numbers 13 and 14 if you need help.

	C	O	L	U	M	N	S
	1	2	3	4	5	6	7
R 1	A	B	C	D	E	F	G
O 2	H	I	J	K	L	M	N
W 3	O	P	R	S	T	U	Y

God told Moses to explore the land of ___ ___ ___ ___ ___ ___
13 11 27 11 11 27

by sending one leader from each ___ ___ ___ ___ ___.
35 33 22 12 15

These men returned after ___ ___ ___ ___ ___ days.
16 31 33 5 37

They said the land flowed with ___ ___ ___ ___ and
26 22 25 24

___ ___ ___ ___ ___. But ten men said,
21 31 27 15 37

"The people are ___ ___ ___ ___ ___ ___ ___ ___ than we are."
34 35 33 31 27 17 15 33

___ ___ ___ ___ ___ ___ and Caleb said,
23 31 34 21 36 11

If the Lord is ___ ___ ___ ___ ___ ___ ___ with us,
32 25 15 11 34 15 14

he will ___ ___ ___ ___ us into that land."
25 15 11 14

 Through the Bible Puzzles, © 2001 by Standard Publishing • Permission granted to photocopy for classroom use only.

Thirst Aid

Begin with the letter M at the top, on the right. Write that M on the first blank below. Then print every other letter on the blanks below, crossing out each letter as you use it. When you reach the center of the circle, go back to the outside of the circle and print the letters you have not yet used. Read Numbers 20:11.

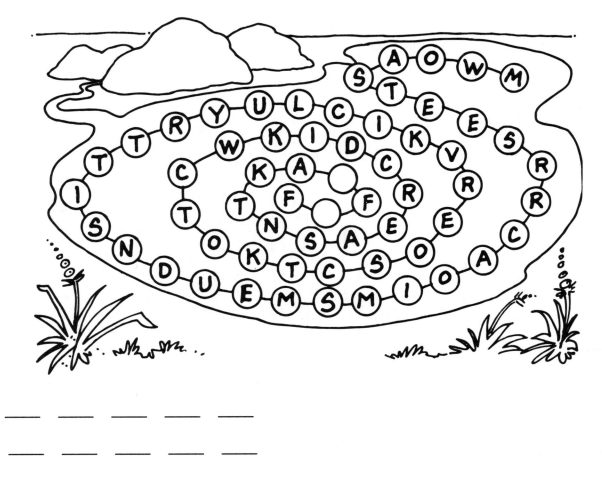

Then ____ ____ ____ ____ ____

____ ____ ____ ____ ____ ____

his arm and ____ ____ ____ ____ ____ ____ the

____ ____ ____ ____ ____ ____ ____ ____ ____ ____ ____

with his ____ ____ ____ ____ ____ .

____ ____ ____ ____ ____ gushed out, and

the ____ ____ ____ ____ ____ ____ ____ ____ ____ and

their ____ ____ ____ ____ ____ ____ ____ ____ ____ ____

____ ____ ____ ____ ____ .

But Why, Lord?

In Deuteronomy 5:1-4, 22-29, read the exciting story of God giving the Ten Commandments. God wants all people to keep his commandments. Use the alphabet below to find out why we should follow God's law.

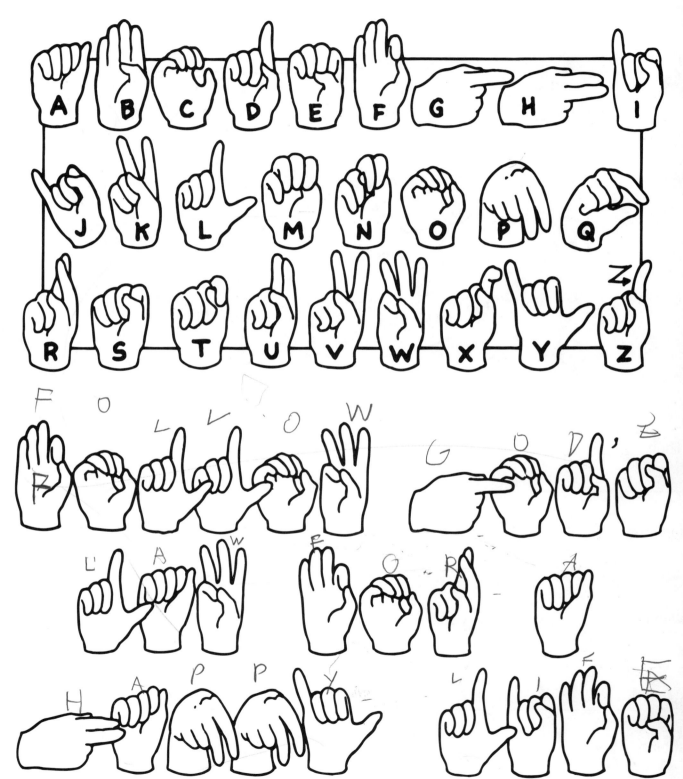

Through the Bible Puzzles, © 2001 by Standard Publishing • Permission granted to photocopy for classroom use only.

Do It Right

In the first row of letters, cross out the letters of the word REMEMBER. In the second row, cross out the letters of the word THE. Continue in this way for each row. Write the leftover letters at the end of each row. They will spell a message.
Example: SHARE. . . S L H A O V E R E = LOVE

REMEMBER . . . . . . R E M L E M O V B E R E ___ ___ ___ ___

THE . . . . T T H E H E ___ ___ ___

LAWS . . . . L L A O W R S D ___ ___ ___ ___

AND . . . . A Y O N D U R ___ ___ ___ ___

DECREES . . . . D E C G O R E E D S ___ ___ ___

OF . . . . W O I F T H ___ ___ ___ ___

MOSES . . . . M A L L O S E S ___ ___ ___

TALK . . . . T A Y O L K U R ___ ___ ___ ___

ABOUT . . . . H E A B O U A R T T ___ ___ ___ ___ ___

THEM . . . . A T N H D E W M I T H ___ ___ ___ ___   ___ ___ ___ ___

THESE . . . . T A L L H E S E ___ ___ ___

COMMANDMENTS . C O Y M O M A N D M U R E N T S ___ ___ ___ ___

ARE . . . . A S R O E U L ___ ___ ___ ___

TO . . . . A N T D W O I T H ___ ___ ___   ___ ___ ___ ___

BE . . . . B A L L E ___ ___ ___

UPON . . . . Y O U U P O R N ___ ___ ___ ___

YOUR . . . . Y S T R O U E N G R T H ___ ___ ___ ___ ___

HEART . . . . H E D E U A T R E R O N O T M Y 6:5

___ ___ ___ ___ ___ ___ ___ ___ ___ ___ ___ ___ ___ ___ ___ ___   ___ : ___

Through the Bible Puzzles, © 2001 by Standard Publishing • Permission granted to photocopy for classroom use only.

Welcome Home

Read Joshua 3:9-17. Then answer the following questions Yes or No.
To find the answer to the last sentence, fold this page so that the arrow at A and B meet the points at A and B. Then write the answer on the line below.

A→   A•

Now the Israelites told Joshua to
listen to the words of
the Lord. _____

The priests were told to car-r-ry
the ark as they
cros-s-s-s-s-s-s-s-s-s-s-s-sssed
the Jordan River. _____

One thing to remember is the Jordan
was at flood stage at this
time. _____

The Israelites
did not want to car-r-r-r-r-ry
the ark. _____

The
group (the Israelites) walked around
the Jordan River.
B→   B•

  Through the Bible Puzzles, © 2001 by Standard Publishing • Permission granted to photocopy for classroom use only.

Shout!

To find the answers to this puzzle, start at the circled letter on the grid below and move, one letter at a time, in the direction shown by the arrows on the line above.
Example: the first line begins with J so find the J in the grid below, then follow the arrow up to the O. From the O, follow the arrow up to the S. Fill in each letter in the line. Read Joshua 6 to find out more about the story.

Who did God call to lead the Israelites after Moses died?

J __ __ __ __ __

What city did the Israelites march around for 6 days?

J __ __ __ __ __ __

What did seven priests carry in front of the ark?

T __ __ __ __ __ __ __

How many times did the people march around the city on the seventh day?

S __ __ __ __

What did the people do when the priests sounded the trumpet blast?

S __ __ __ __ __ __

What did the wall of the city do when the people shouted?

C __ __ __ __ __ __ __ __

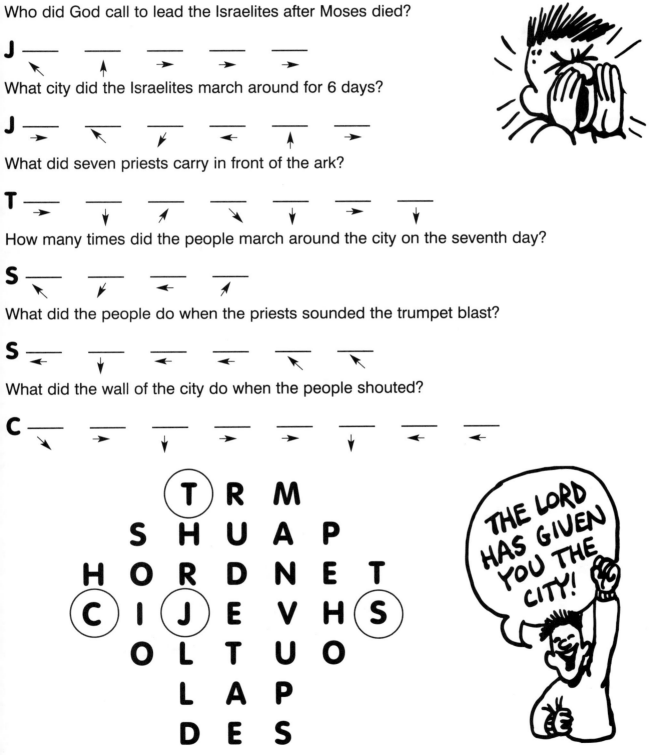

```
        (T)  R   M
     S   H   U   A   P
   H   O   R   D   N   E   T
 (C)  I  (J)  E   V   H  (S)
     O   L   T   U   O
         L   A   P
         D   E   S
```

THE LORD HAS GIVEN YOU THE CITY!

Achan's Sin

Read Joshua 7:16-26; 8:1. These verses tell us that Achan disobeyed God and took some things that did not belong to him. Read the pictures below to discover a very important lesson that Achan learned the hard way.

_ _ _ _ _ _ _ _ _ _ _ _ _ _

_ _ _ _ _ _ _ _ _ _ _ _ _ _

_ _ _ _ _ _ _ _ _ _ _ _ _ _

_ _ _ _ _ _ _ _ _ _ _

Through the Bible Puzzles, © 2001 by Standard Publishing • Permission granted to photocopy for classroom use only.

Remember the Promise

To find Joshua's message, first number the parts of the story in order. Look up Joshua 24:1-18 if you need help. Then use the circled and squared letters to fill in the puzzle message. For example, 1 in a square means H because the squared letter in part 1 of the story is H.

☐	You live⬛d in the desert for a lon⊙g time.	☐ To I⊙s aac I gav⬛e Jacob and Esau.
☐	I sent Moses and Aa⊙r on and brought yo⬛u out of Egypt.	☐ Your ⊙f orefat⬛h ers . . . lived beyond the river.
☐	I led ⊙A braham through⬛o ut Canaan.	☐ I gave you a land on ⊙w hich you did not toi⬛l .
☐	Jacob and his sons went dow⊙n to Egyp⬛t .	☐ To Abraham ⬛I ga⊙v e Isaac.

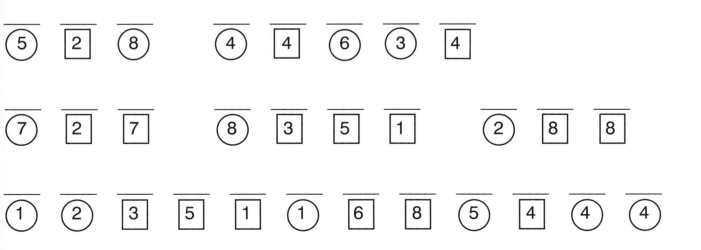

⑤ |2| ⑧   ④ |4| ⑥ ③ |4|

⑦ |2| |7| ⑧ |3| |5| |1| ② |8| |8|

① ② |3| |5| |1| ① |6| |8| ⑤ |4| ④ ④

Lead the Way

Read these statements from Judges 4. If the statement is true, follow the T path. If it is false, follow the F path.

Write the word at the end of each path in the blank space.

1. The Israelites once again did evil (4:1).

2. The Lord sold them into the hands of Jabin (4:2).

3. Jabin cruelly oppressed them for 100 years (4:3).

4. Deborah was leading Israel at that time (4:4).

5. Sisera was the commander of Jabin's army (4:7).

6. Israelites came to Deborah to decide their disputes (4:5).

7. Barak led 10,000 men against Sisera (4:6).

8. Barak said he would never go (4:8).

9. All the troops of Sisera fell by the sword. Only two men were left (4:16).

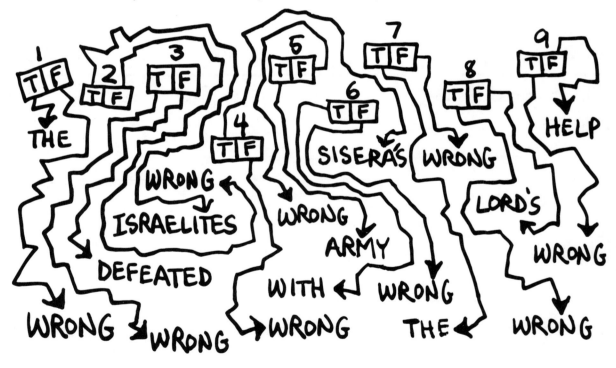

___ ___ ___   ___ ___ ___ ___ ___

___ ___ ___ ___ ___ ___ ___   ___ ___ ___ ___   ___,___

___ ___ ___ ___ ___ ___   ___ ___ ___

___ ___ ___ ___,   ___ ___ ___ ___.

   Through the Bible Puzzles, © 2001 by Standard Publishing • Permission granted to photocopy for classroom use only.

Surprise!

Israel's army was very small, but they followed God's directions. Find their battle cry from Judges 7:20 by filling in the boxes. Each box connects with other boxes that contain the same letter.

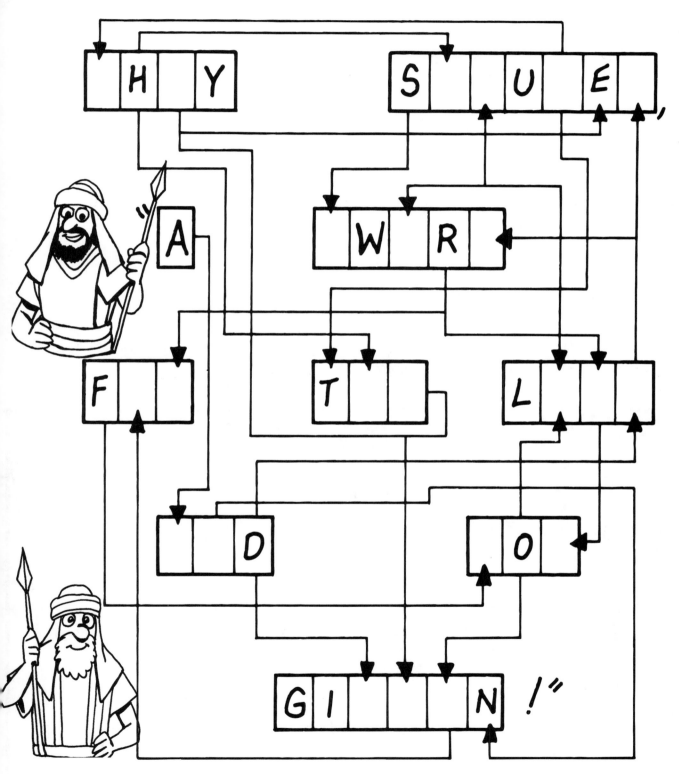

Samson's Weakness

Sixteen words in this story from Judges 13:1 and 16:4-30 have been switched. The front letters of each switched word have been moved to the back. Circle the sixteen switched words, unscramble them, and write them correctly on a sheet of paper.

Samson was born while the Israelites were vessla of the Philistines. He fell in velo with Lilahde. The Philistines asked Delilah to find the retsec of Samson's engthstr.

Samson said, "No orraz has ever been used on my head. If my head were vedsha, my strength would leave."

Delilah shaved off Samson's irha while he was leepas. Samson stlo his strength and the Philistines seized him and put him in sonpri.

Samson was brought out to formper for the Philistines. He yedpra to the Lord for strength.

The Lord heard Samson's prayer, and when Samson pushed the larspil of the pletem, it came down on the rulers and all the people in it.

 Through the Bible Puzzles, © 2001 by Standard Publishing • Permission granted to photocopy for classroom use only.

What a Friend!

Read Ruth 1:1-10 and 14-19 to answer the sentences below. If the sentence is true, circle the letter under the YES column. If it is not true, circle the letter under the NO column. Then fill in the blanks with the circled letters in order from 1–18. Discover what kind of friend Ruth was.

		YES	NO
1.	Naomi wanted Ruth and Orpah to go to their home.	S	P
2.	Elimelech's family went to Bethel.	J	H
3.	His sons'names were Mahlon and Kilion.	E	R
4.	Ruth wanted to leave Naomi and go home.	S	W
5.	Orpah left Naomi and went home.	A	M
6.	Ruth and Orpah were happy to leave Naomi.	N	S
7.	Mahlon and Kilion were Ruth's brothers.	A	L
8.	Elimelech moved his family because of a famine.	O	H
9.	Ruth and Orpah were from Bethlehem.	U	Y
10.	Ruth stayed with Naomi.	A	B
11.	Ruth and Naomi went to Bethlehem.	L	R
12.	Naomi, Ruth, and Orpah went to Moab when they inherited money.	J	T
13.	Elimelech was from Bethlehem in the land of Judah.	O	A
14.	Ruth and Orpah were Naomi's daughters–in–law.	N	P
15.	Ruth wanted to follow a different God than Naomi.	U	A
16.	This story happened in the days when the kings ruled.	L	O
17.	Elimelech, Mahlon, and Kilion died.	M	B
18.	Naomi heard in Moab that the Lord had come to the aid of his people.	I	C

— — — — — — — — — — — — — — — — — — .

Here I Am!

In 1 Samuel 3:1-20, the Lord called to Samuel. Read these verses to find out how Samuel answered the Lord. Then begin with the word "Speak" in the puzzle and find the path that matches Samuel's answer. Do not trace any line in the puzzle more than once, and change directions only at intersections marked by dots.

 Through the Bible Puzzles, © 2001 by Standard Publishing • Permission granted to photocopy for classroom use only.

Sounds Like . . .

In these statements from 1 Samuel 8–10, the correct word has been replaced with a rhyming word. Find the rhyming words and write them in the "across" shapes below. Then write the correct words in the "down" shapes.

1.   The Israelites wanted a ring (8:5).

2.   God said, "Listen to them and live them a king" (8:22).

3.   The Lord told Samuel he would send a can from the land of Benjamin (9:16).

4.   "Anoint him reader over my people Israel" (9:16).

5.   Samuel took a flask of soil and poured it on Saul's head (10:1).

6.   "He will deliver my steeple from the hand of the Philistines" (9:16).

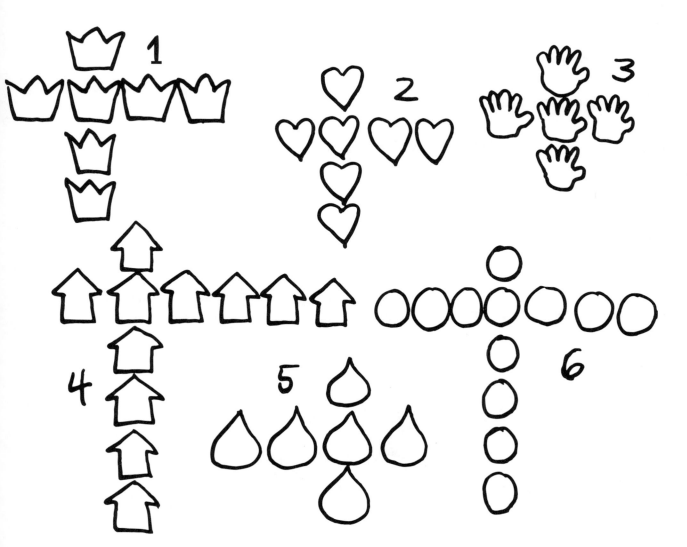

Look Inside

Look inside each of these sentences to find a hidden word. Hidden words are between other words, such as the word "egg" in this sentence: (2) Peg gave out cookies. The number 2 means that the hidden word starts with the second letter from the beginning of the sentence. (If you want to make the puzzle harder, cover up the number clues.) The blanks after each sentence show how many letters the hidden word has. Read 1 Samuel 16:1-13 to learn more about Samuel's mission.

(11)   Mary went with Ed to the park. _____ _____ _____

(6)   The color does not match. _____ _____ _____ _____

(8)   We ate nachos every day. _____ _____ _____ _____ _____

(9)   I will send a videotape. _____ _____ _____ _____ _____

(5)   Pam is one of my best friends. _____ _____ _____

(2)   Go for a walk before it rains. _____ _____

(1)   Jess earned straight As. _____ _____ _____ _____ _____

(3)   Not one piece of mail came today. _____ _____

(3)   Rob enjoyed the baseball game. _____ _____

(9)   A big pumpkin grows slowly. _____ _____ _____ _____

(8)   Please move Randy's bike. _____ _____ _____ _____

(1)   Is Rae lending her book? _____ _____ _____ _____ _____

   Through the Bible Puzzles, © 2001 by Standard Publishing • Permission granted to photocopy for classroom use only.

Stones 'n Stuff

After reading 1 Samuel 17:40-51, fill in the answers to each sentence. Then use the letters above the numbers to fill in the coded message in each stone.

1. David put the stones in a pouch of his _ _ _ _ _ _ _ _ '_ _ $\frac{}{2}$ _ (v. 40).

$\frac{}{5}$

2. Goliath was a _ _ $\frac{}{13}$ _ _ _ $\frac{}{3}$ _ $\frac{}{7}$ _ (v. 40).

3. Goliath despised David for he was only a _ $\frac{}{11}$ _ (v. 42).

4. Goliath had a $\frac{}{14}$ _ _ _ _ , _ _ _ _ _ and

   _ _ _ $\frac{}{4}$ _ _ _ to fight David (v. 45).

5. David came to fight Goliath in the name of the _ _ $\frac{}{9}$ _ _ _ _ _ _ $\frac{}{8}$ _ _ _

   (v. 45).

6. All those gathered here will $\frac{}{6}$ _ _ $\frac{}{12}$ that it is not by sword or spear that the Lord

   saves (v. 47).

7. David struck the Philistine on the _ _ _ _ $\frac{}{10}$ _ _ _ (v. 49).

8. After David _ _ $\frac{}{1}$ _ _ _ him, he cut off his head with the sword (v. 51).

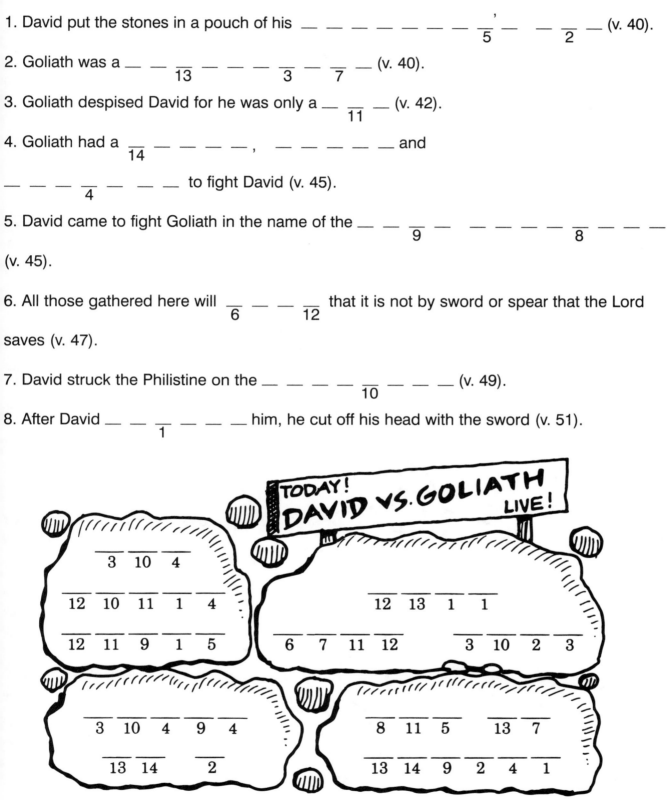

TODAY!
DAVID VS. GOLIATH LIVE!

Stone 1:
$\overline{3}$ $\overline{10}$ $\overline{4}$
$\overline{12}$ $\overline{10}$ $\overline{11}$ $\overline{1}$ $\overline{4}$
$\overline{12}$ $\overline{11}$ $\overline{9}$ $\overline{1}$ $\overline{5}$

Stone 2:
$\overline{12}$ $\overline{13}$ $\overline{1}$ $\overline{1}$
$\overline{6}$ $\overline{7}$ $\overline{11}$ $\overline{12}$ $\overline{3}$ $\overline{10}$ $\overline{2}$ $\overline{3}$

Stone 3:
$\overline{3}$ $\overline{10}$ $\overline{4}$ $\overline{9}$ $\overline{4}$
$\overline{13}$ $\overline{14}$ $\overline{2}$

Stone 4:
$\overline{8}$ $\overline{11}$ $\overline{5}$ $\overline{13}$ $\overline{7}$
$\overline{13}$ $\overline{14}$ $\overline{9}$ $\overline{2}$ $\overline{4}$ $\overline{1}$

Friends Forever

Trace the path to each star to find the scrambled words. Then fill in the sentences about the story from 1 Samuel 19, 20, and 2 Samuel 9.

1. Saul told Jonathan to ___ ___ ___ ___ David.

2. Jonathan ___ ___ ___ ___ ___ ___ David that Saul wanted to kill David.

3. Jonathan ___ ___ ___ ___ ___ his friend David.

4. They swore ___ ___ ___ ___ ___ ___ ___ ___ ___ ___ with each other in

   the name of the Lord.

5. When David became king, he rewarded the ___ ___ ___ of Jonathan for his father's

   kindness.

 Through the Bible Puzzles, © 2001 by Standard Publishing • Permission granted to photocopy for classroom use only.

Have Mercy on Me!

Unscramble the bold letters at the top of the box to spell the name of a main character from 1 Samuel 24:1-17. Then write the bold letters in the correct order in the top of the empty box. Take the columns that appear under each bold letter and write them under the same letter in the empty box. When completed, read from left to right to see what this character said to show mercy.

V	D	I	D	A
Lord	May	judge	between	the
me.	you	And	may	and
avenge	the	the	wrongs	Lord
done	you	to	me,	have
hand	but	will	not	my
	touch			you.

The Wise King

One word is missing from each of these statements from 1 Kings 3:5-15. Color the spaces containing any of the letters K, I, N, G, or S to find the missing words.

1. The Lord appeared to _____ in a dream (3:5).

K	S	K	E	I	N	I	Q	G	Z	A	B	S	K	I	Q	N	W	P	E	K	Q	K	I	N	V	I	A	Q	S
I	C	P	F	N	M	K	R	S	Y	C	Q	G	M	N	R	G	N	C	S	I	P	I	R	G	W	G	K	C	G
N	G	S	H	G	O	S	T	K	X	E	F	N	O	G	T	S	X	G	F	N	O	K	T	S	X	K	P	S	N
A	Q	K	J	S	P	G	U	I	W	H	J	I	P	S	U	K	Y	B	H	G	M	I	U	K	Y	S	E	F	I
G	N	I	L	K	I	N	V	N	G	S	L	K	I	K	V	I	Z	A	J	S	L	N	G	S	Z	N	H	J	K

2. Solomon asked God for a discerning _____ (3:9).

K	A	I	E	I	I	I	Q	S	K	I	Z	K	I	N	L	G	S	K
G	Q	N	F	N	M	O	R	G	W	N	A	I	E	G	M	V	I	W
I	K	G	H	G	G	G	T	N	I	G	B	N	K	S	O	U	N	X
S	C	S	J	S	O	P	U	K	X	S	C	G	I	H	P	T	N	Y
N	D	K	L	K	K	K	V	I	Y	K	D	S	F	N	Q	R	I	Z

3. The Lord was _____ (3:10).

K	I	N	R	K	T	X	Y	S	K	I	E	K	N	G	L	N	I	K	R	S	K	I	A	N	S	K	O
I	E	G	Q	K	U	Y	Z	G	C	P	F	S	H	N	M	G	P	Q	T	N	Y	Z	B	I	H	M	I
N	I	S	P	K	V	Z	A	N	I	K	D	I	G	I	O	S	K	I	U	I	S	K	C	K	J	P	N
G	F	J	O	I	W	X	B	I	A	B	E	N	J	S	P	L	O	N	V	G	X	D	E	S	L	Q	K
S	H	L	M	I	N	N	C	K	S	N	F	G	H	K	M	K	S	G	W	K	I	S	F	G	N	I	R

4. God also promised Solomon _____, _____, and a _____ _____ (3:13, 14).

S	K	I	N	H	K	X	S	K	I	H	N	P	K	Q	G	G	S	B	N	I	K
I	A	B	G	J	I	Y	G	A	B	J	G	Q	S	R	S	V	U	C	G	Z	A
K	I	K	S	L	N	X	N	C	D	L	S	N	G	T	K	I	N	D	S	K	I
N	C	N	F	H	G	Z	I	E	F	M	K	R	I	U	I	T	A	E	X	Y	N
G	D	E	G	J	S	L	K	I	N	O	I	P	N	V	N	G	S	F	I	S	G

G	A	K	E	K	K	K	Q	S	T	X	N	A	I	G	G	L	K	K	I	N
I	B	I	F	I	M	S	R	N	I	Z	S	B	K	F	G	M	I	A	B	G
S	G	N	H	N	O	G	X	S	U	S	N	C	K	H	G	O	N	K	I	S
K	C	I	J	G	P	N	Y	K	V	Y	K	D	I	J	N	P	G	C	N	D
I	D	K	L	S	K	I	Z	S	W	X	S	E	N	S	S	Q	S	E	F	G

K	A	B	C	N	G	N	A	S	F	M	I	R	K	I	N	G	H	K	A	B	C	I	O	N	S	K	A	I	K	I
I	D	E	F	G	R	G	Q	K	S	O	N	T	S	Z	A	B	C	I	X	Y	Z	K	P	G	U	V	Q	N	F	H
K	H	J	L	N	T	N	C	I	H	K	G	U	K	Y	G	N	F	N	T	U	V	S	Q	S	N	G	C	G	G	S
I	M	O	P	G	U	G	D	N	J	P	S	V	I	X	D	I	E	G	W	X	Y	G	R	K	W	X	D	S	J	L
K	I	K	Q	N	G	N	E	G	L	Q	K	W	N	G	S	K	J	S	K	I	D	N	T	I	Y	Z	E	K	I	N

Through the Bible Puzzles, © 2001 by Standard Publishing • Permission granted to photocopy for classroom use only.

Good Advice

The elders and the young men gave King Rehoboam advice. Unscramble the letters on each man to make a word. Then fill in the blanks to find the advice each group gave. Read 1 Kings 12 to find out who Rehoboam listened to.

Elders

___ ___ ___ ___ them a ___ ___ ___ ___ ___ ___ ___ ___ ___

___ ___ ___ ___ ___ ___ (12:7).

Young men

Tell them you will make their ___ ___ ___ ___

___ ___ ___ ___ ___ ___ ___ ___ ___ ___ (12:10, 11).

Through the Bible Puzzles, © 2001 by Standard Publishing • Permission granted to photocopy for classroom use only.

Help From on High

In 1 Kings 17:1-6, God helped Elijah when he hid from the king. Cross out all the Cs, Gs, Ks, Os and Qs in the stream. Then rearrange the remaining letters to find three things God provided for Elijah.

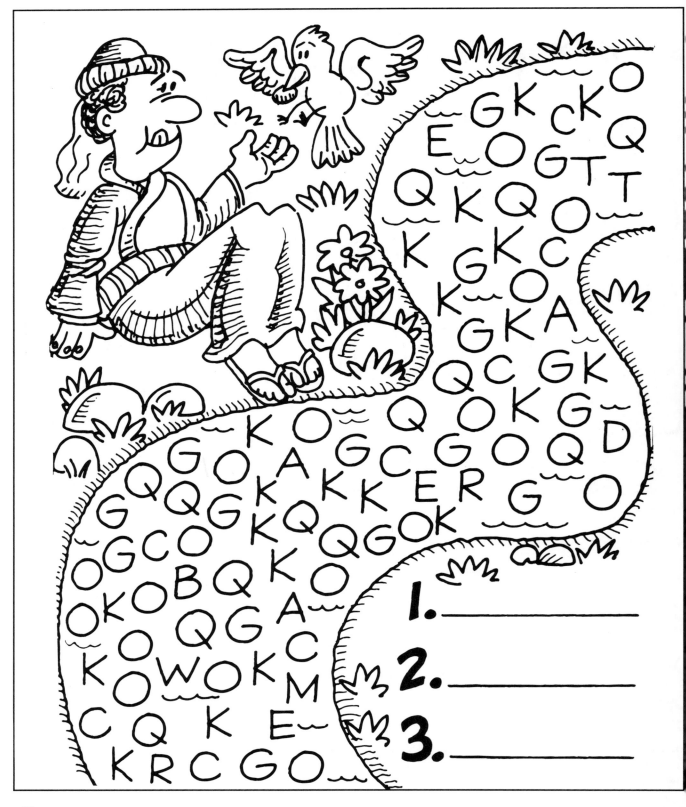

1. _____

2. _____

3. _____

 Through the Bible Puzzles, © 2001 by Standard Publishing • Permission granted to photocopy for classroom use only.

Rescue Recipe

God sent Elijah to a widow who fed him during a terrible famine. To find the recipe for the widow's food, unscramble the letters in the matching jars. Read 1 Kings 17:7-16 to find out how Elijah helped the widow.

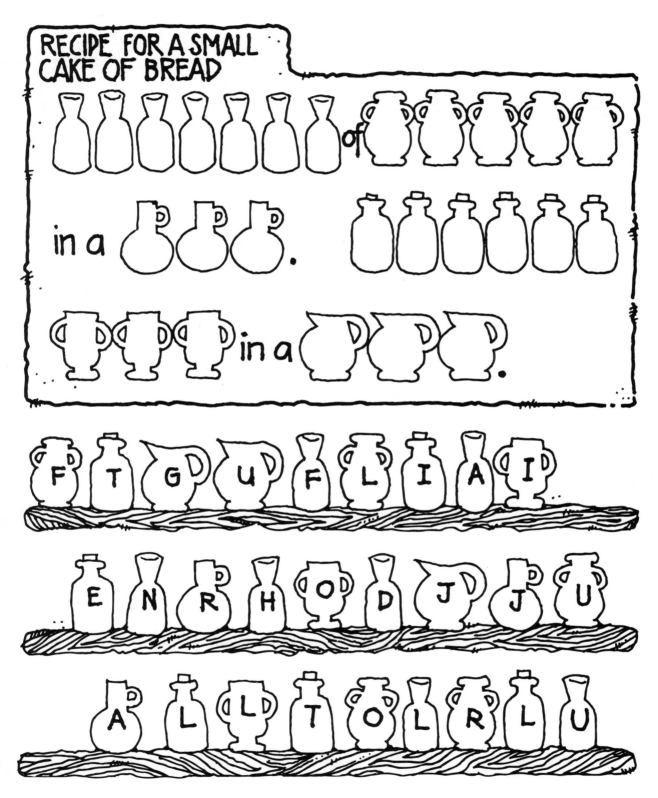

Through the Bible Puzzles, © 2001 by Standard Publishing • Permission granted to photocopy for classroom use only.

And the Winner Is . . .

Find the box marked A1 at the top of the page. Copy what you see in the box into the empty A1 square in the grid. Fill in the other squares. (Or, cut the squares at the top of the page apart and paste them in their proper places.) Read 1 Kings 18:20-39 to learn about Elijah's contest.

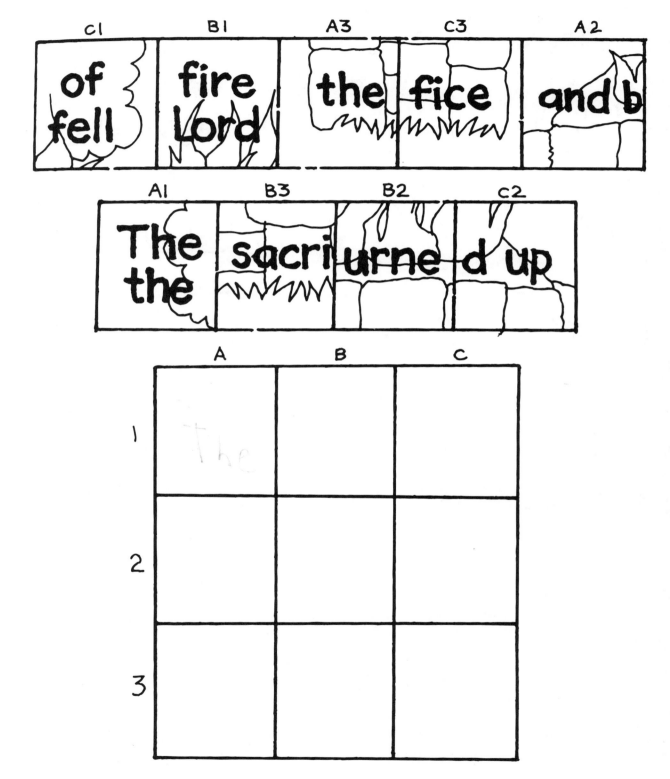

Through the Bible Puzzles, © 2001 by Standard Publishing • Permission granted to photocopy for classroom use only.

Whirlwind Words

Read about the whirlwind in 2 Kings 2:1-11. Then connect the words from the story to follow Elijah's path to Heaven.

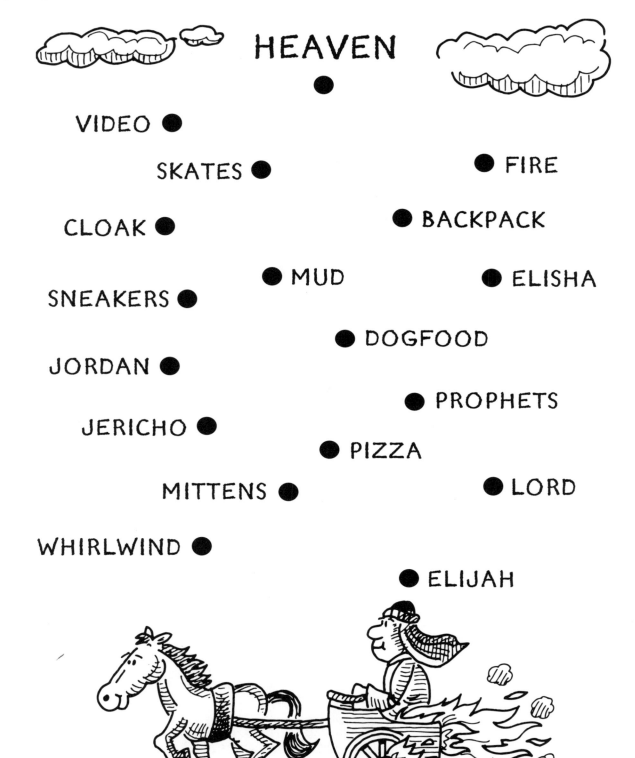

HEAVEN

VIDEO

SKATES

FIRE

CLOAK

BACKPACK

SNEAKERS

MUD

ELISHA

DOGFOOD

JORDAN

PROPHETS

JERICHO

PIZZA

MITTENS

LORD

WHIRLWIND

ELIJAH

Through the Bible Puzzles, © 2001 by Standard Publishing • Permission granted to photocopy for classroom use only.

What a Blessing!

To find out how Elisha helped a family, read 2 Kings 4:8-10, 17-22, and 32-37. Then read the sentences below. The sketch in each blank resembles a letter of the alphabet. Can you guess which letters? Then think of a word suggested by the sketches that fit the blanks.

1. A well-to-do woman asked Elisha to stay for a ____ ____ [cup] [knife] (v. 8).

2. The woman and her husband made a room on the roof and put in it a bed, a table, a

____ [chair] ____ ____ ____ , and a lamp for Elisha (v. 10).

3. The woman gave birth to a ____ [boy face] ____ (v. 17).

4. The boy sat on his mother's lap until ____ [clock] [clock] ____ and then died (v. 20).

5. When Elisha reached the [house] [window] ____ ____ ____, the boy was lying dead on

his couch (v. 32).

6. Elisha laid upon the boy, mouth to mouth, [eye] ____ [eye] ____ to eyes, hands to

hands (v. 34).

7. The boy ____ [a-h choo! nose] ____ ____ ____ ____ ____ seven times and opened his eyes

(v.35).

8. Elisha said to Gehazi, " [phone] ____ ____ ____ the Shunammite" (v. 36).

9. When Elisha told the woman to take her son, she fell at his [blow dryer] ____ ____ ____

(v. 37).

 Through the Bible Puzzles, © 2001 by Standard Publishing • Permission granted to photocopy for classroom use only.

Who Said That?

Read 2 Kings 5:1-14. Then complete the printed letters by drawing a straight line between the cross or circle at the top of the space and its matching cross or circle. Then match what is said with the person who said it.

____ "If only my master would see the prophet who is in Samaria!"

____ "Am I God? Can I kill and bring back to life?"

____ "Go, wash yourself seven times in the Jordan, and your flesh will be restored and you

will be cleansed."

____ "Are not Abana and Pharpar, the rivers of Damascus, better than any of the waters of

Israel?"

____ "By all means, go."

Through the Bible Puzzles, © 2001 by Standard Publishing • Permission granted to photocopy for classroom use only.

Bad Shape

Captured by their enemies, the Israelites were in bad SHAPE. To learn why, match the shapes underneath each blank with the letter shapes above. Write the letters on the blanks. Read 2 Kings 17 to find out more about the story.

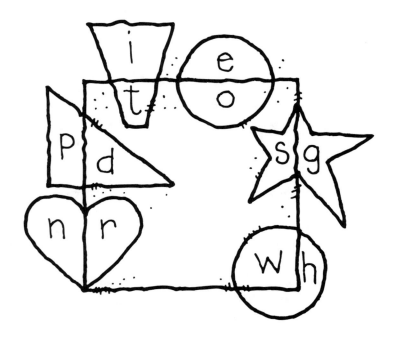

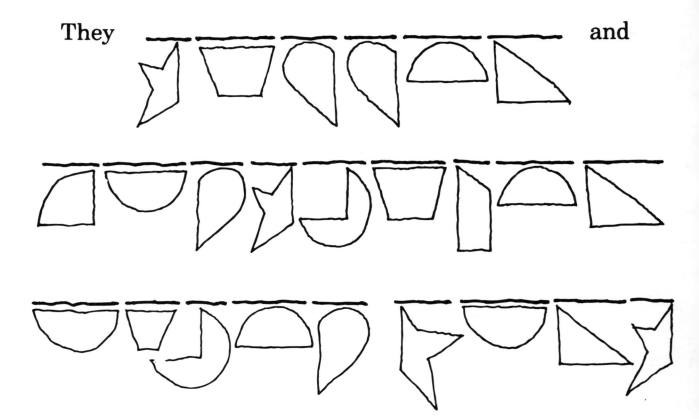

They ___ ___ ___ ___ ___ ___ and

 Through the Bible Puzzles, © 2001 by Standard Publishing • Permission granted to photocopy for classroom use only.

What Was Their Downfall?

Read 2 Kings 17:7-18. Start with the circle that is numbered the same as the sentence and follow the arrows to fill in the blanks. When completed, you will find some bad things Israel did to cause their downfall with God.

1. The Israelites had ___ ___ ___ ___ ___ ___ against the Lord their God.

2. They followed the ___ ___ ___ ___ ___ ___ ___ ___ ___ of the nations the Lord had driven out.

3. They built themselves ___ ___ ___ ___ places in all their towns.

4. They set up sacred ___ ___ ___ ___ ___ ___ and poles.

5. The did ___ ___ ___ ___ ___ ___ things that provoked the Lord to anger.

6. They worshiped ___ ___ ___ ___ ___ .

7. They would not listen and were as ___ ___ ___ ___ ___ ___ ___ ___ ___ ___ ___ as their fathers.

8. They ___ ___ ___ ___ ___ ___ ___ ___ his decrees and covenant.

9. They became ___ ___ ___ ___ ___ ___ ___ ___ ___ .

10. They provoked the Lord to ___ ___ ___ ___ ___ .

Our God Is Greater

Read the verses given after each statement from 2 Chronicles to complete these statements. Use the numbered letters in your answers to fill in the puzzle message about God.

Solomon gave orders to ___ ___ ___ ___ ___ a
                               5   6

___ ___ ___ ___ ___ ___ for the ___ ___ ___ ___ of the
     1   2   10

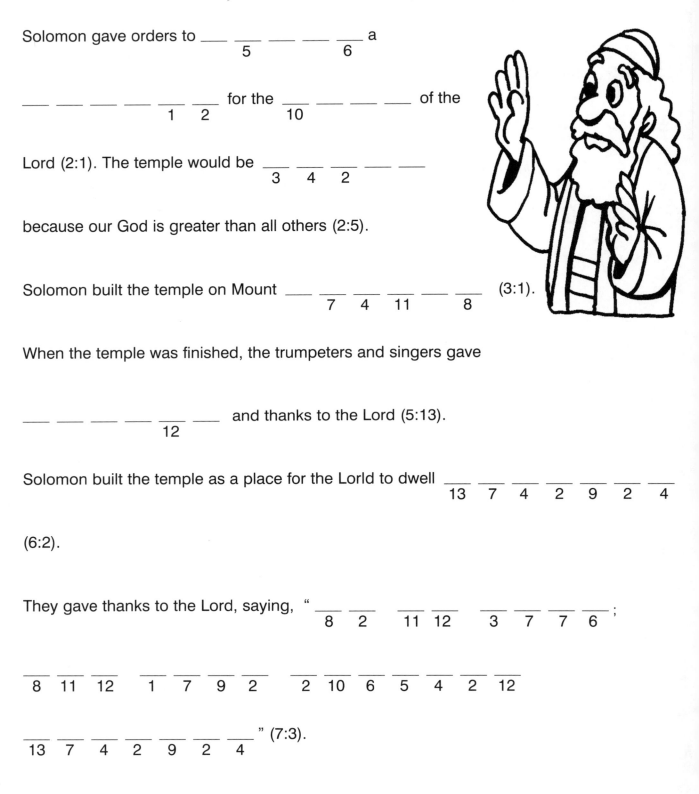

Lord (2:1). The temple would be ___ ___ ___ ___ ___
                                  3   4   2

because our God is greater than all others (2:5).

Solomon built the temple on Mount ___ ___ ___ ___ ___ ___ (3:1).
                                    7   4   11   8

When the temple was finished, the trumpeters and singers gave

___ ___ ___ ___ ___ ___ and thanks to the Lord (5:13).
             12

Solomon built the temple as a place for the Lorld to dwell ___ ___ ___ ___ ___ ___ ___
                                                            13   7   4   2   9   2   4

(6:2).

They gave thanks to the Lord, saying, " ___ ___ ___ ___ ___ ___ ___ ___ ;
                                         8   2   11 12   3   7   7   6

___ ___ ___ ___ ___ ___ ___ ___ ___ ___ ___ ___ ___
 8 11 12   1   7   9   2   2 10   6   5   4   2 12

___ ___ ___ ___ ___ ___ ___ " (7:3).
13   7   4   2   9   2   4

     Through the Bible Puzzles, © 2001 by Standard Publishing • Permission granted to photocopy for classroom use only.

Work Boxes

Fill in the work boxes by following the instructions below. Read 2 Chronicles 24:1-14 to learn how the people gave.

Boxes

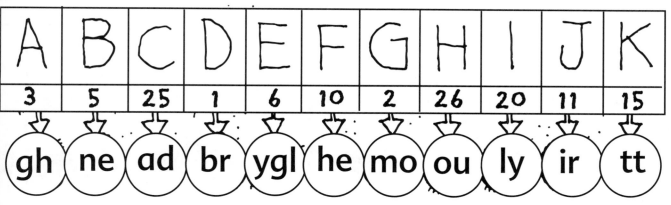

Write the number answers in the small rectangle work boxes.

1. Add boxes **A**, **B**, and **G**. Place the total in work box **E**.
2. Subtract box **B** from box **C**. Place the answer in work box **K**.
3. Add boxes **C** and **D**. Place the total in work box **B**.
4. Subtract box **A** from box **B**. Place the answer in work box **G**.
5. Add boxes **B** and **E**. Place the total in work box **F**.
6. Subtract box **G** from box **A**. Place the answer in work box **A**.
7. Subtract box **J** from box **H**. Place the answer in work box **D**.
8. Subtract box **B** from box **J**. Place the answer in work box **I** .
9. Add boxes **G** and **D**. Place the total in work box **C**.
10. Add boxes **B** and **I**. Place the total in work box **J**.
11. Subtract box **K** from box **I**. Place the answer in work box **H**.

In the circles below each work box, write the letters shown below the same number at the top of the page.

Work Boxes

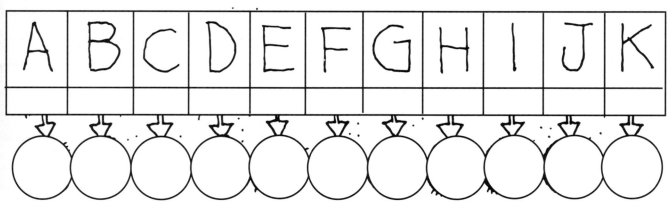

Through the Bible Puzzles, © 2001 by Standard Publishing • Permission granted to photocopy for classroom use only.

The Secret of Success

Uzziah became king when he was only 16 years old, yet he was a successful and powerful ruler for many years. How did he do it? Use these charts to find out. At the top of each column, write the letter indicated by the black square in the box. (See 2 Chronicles 26:1-5.)

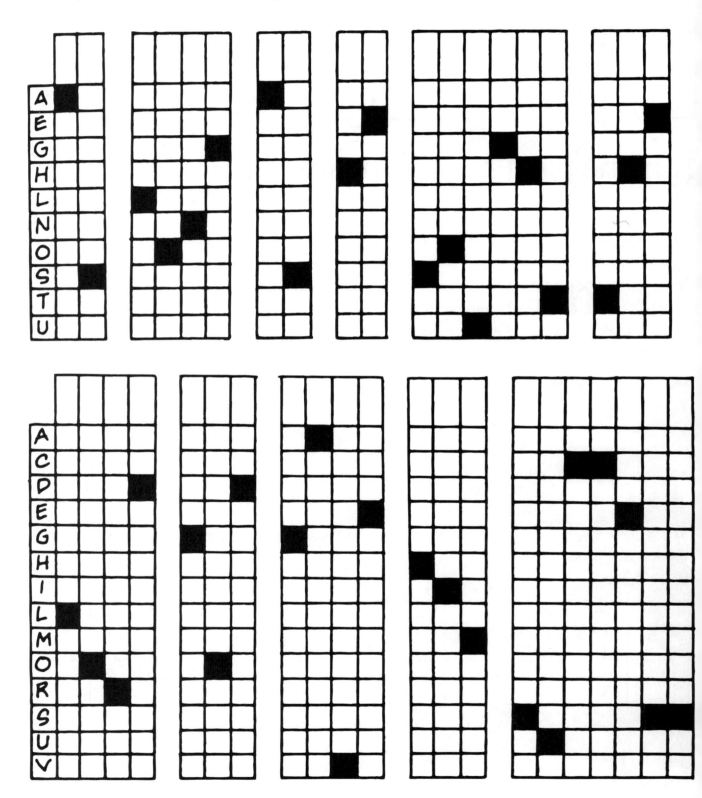

Through the Bible Puzzles, © 2001 by Standard Publishing • Permission granted to photocopy for classroom use only.

Construction Site

How did the Israelites rebuild the city wall? To find out, look at the wall below. For each white brick, find the brick that exactly matches it in the code key. Write the letter in the matching blank brick. Read Nehemiah 6:15, 16 if you need help.

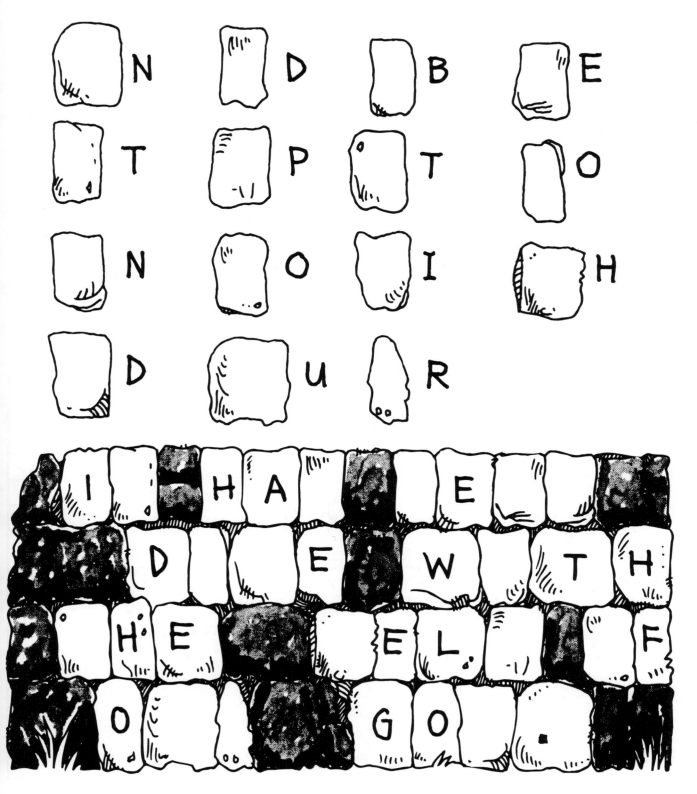

A Brave Queen

The Jews in Susa were in danger. If Queen Esther tried to save her people, she might be killed. To find out what Esther decided, decode the message below. Read more about what happened in Esther 4—8:8.

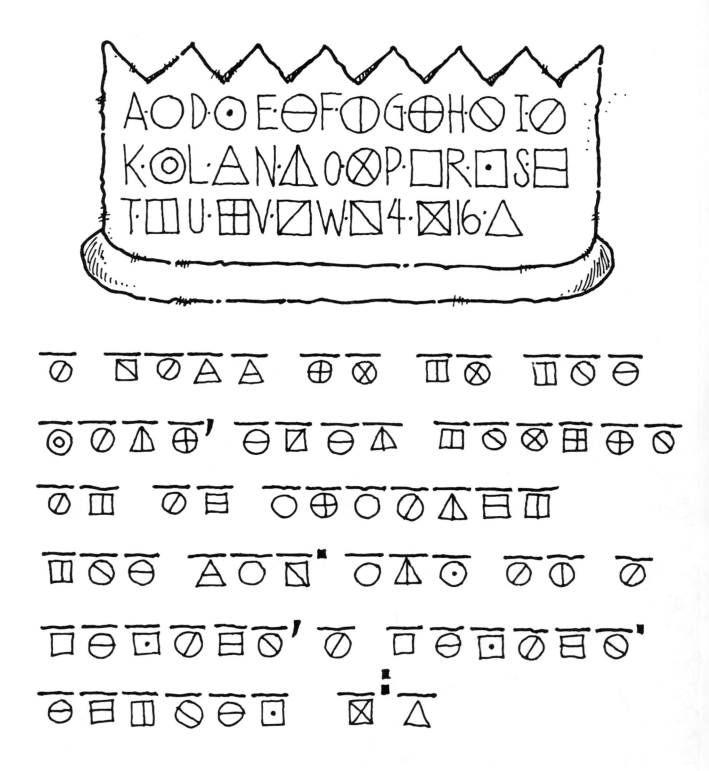

Through the Bible Puzzles, © 2001 by Standard Publishing • Permission granted to photocopy for classroom use only.

Why Me?

Read Job 38:1-11; 42:1-3. God asked Job some questions to show Job who God really is. Use a pencil to color in each square that contains a question mark. When completed, you will find Job's answer about God.

Through the Bible Puzzles, © 2001 by Standard Publishing • Permission granted to photocopy for classroom use only.

Lost Sheep

Help the sheep find the shepherd. Find the misspelled letter in each sheep's name taken from Psalm 23. Put the correct letter in the blank below with the same number.

Who is our shepherd? __G__ __o__ __d__ _____ _____ _____ _____
　　　　　　　　　　　　　　1　　　2　　　3　　　4　　　5　　　6　　　7

1 pashures

2 stadow

3 grean

4 soup

5 ail

6 watems

7 gootness

 Through the Bible Puzzles, © 2001 by Standard Publishing • Permission granted to photocopy for classroom use only.

Wise Up!

Wise King Solomon had a very important job. Read Proverbs 23:19-21, 29, and 24:1, 2 for clues to complete the picture. If a statement below is true, move the number of spaces given. If the statement is false, do not move. Use a marker or crayon to make a thick line as you follow the directions.

Begin at the large dot near the northwest corner.

1. If we are to listen, move **9** spaces south.
2. If we are to be wise, move **13** spaces east.
3. If we are to keep our hearts on the right path, move **2** spaces north.
4. If we are to join those who drink too much wine, move **3** spaces northeast.
5. If gluttons become poor, move **13** spaces west.
6. If there are six questions in verse **29**, move **7** spaces north.
7. If we are asked who has sorrow, move **3** spaces southeast.
8. If we are to envy wicked men, move **2** spaces southwest.
9. If we are not to desire wicked men's company, move **3½** spaces northeast.
10. If wicked men's hearts plot violence, move **3½** spaces southeast.
11. If wicked men's lips talk about making trouble, move **3** spaces northeast.
12. If Solomon is telling us to "Wise Up," move **9** spaces south.

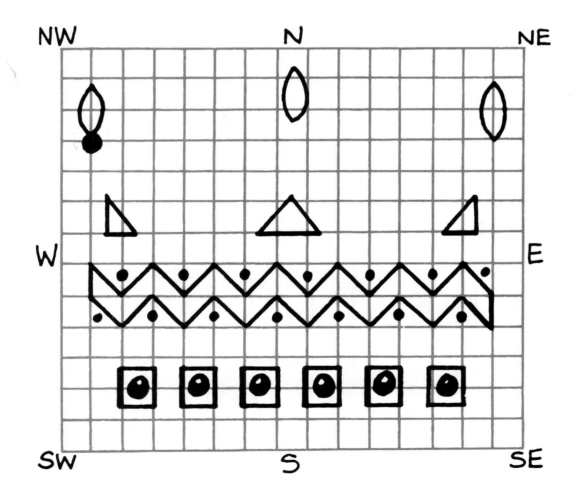

When the Lord Calls

What did Isaiah say when he heard the voice of the Lord calling for someone to do God's work? Isaiah's answer, which should be our answer too, is hidden in this puzzle. Color all the spaces containing a dot to make the answer appear.

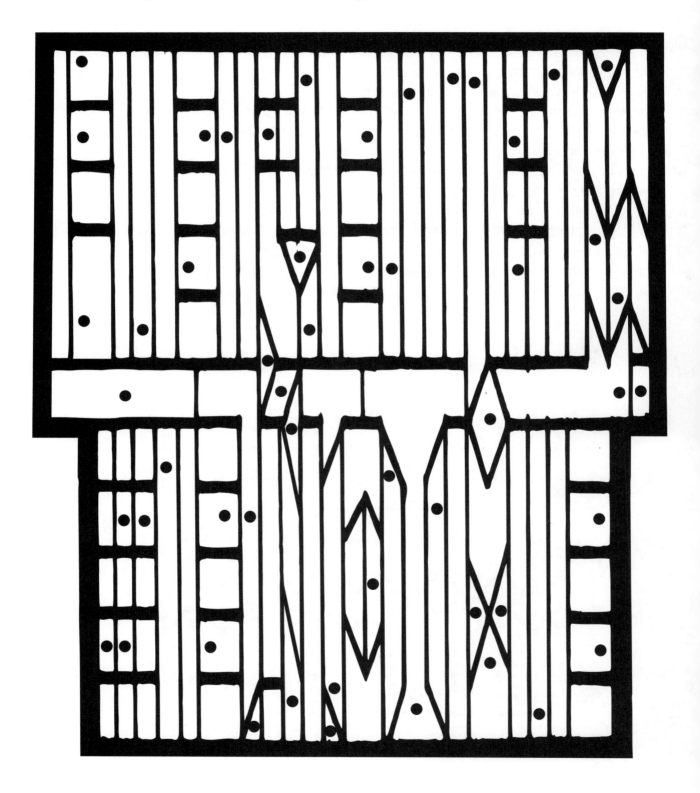

 Through the Bible Puzzles, © 2001 by Standard Publishing • Permission granted to photocopy for classroom use only.

His Name Is . . .

Cross out every b, j, k, q, x, and z to discover the names for Jesus in Isaiah 9:6 and Luke 1:32-35. Write the names below.

W	B	O	J	N	K	D	Q	E	X	R	Z	F
U	L	Z	C	X	O	U	K	N	Q	S	E	L
O	J	R	B	M	K	I	G	X	H	T	Z	Y
G	O	X	D	B	E	J	V	K	E	Q	R	L
A	S	Z	T	I	Q	N	B	G	J	F	K	A
T	Q	H	B	E	J	R	K	P	R	X	I	N
Z	C	E	O	X	F	P	E	X	A	C	Z	E
S	B	O	J	N	K	O	Q	F	T	Z	H	E
M	O	Z	S	J	T	B	H	K	I	Q	G	H
S	O	X	N	O	F	K	G	J	O	B	D	Q

Isaiah 9:6

1. __ __ __ __ __ __ __ __ __   __ __ __ __ __ __ __ __ __ __ __

2. __ __ __ __ __ __ __   __ __ __ __

3. __ __ __ __ __ __ __ __ __   __ __ __ __ __ __ __

4. __ __ __ __ __   __ __   __ __ __ __ __

Luke 1

5. __ __ __   __ __   __ __ __   __ __ __ __ __ __   __ __ __ __ __

6. __ __ __   __ __   __ __ __ __

Through the Bible Puzzles, © 2001 by Standard Publishing • Permission granted to photocopy for classroom use only.

Missing Alphabet

The missing letter in each alphabet puzzle tells us of the greatness of God. Discover which letter of the alphabet is missing from each line and write it on the spaces below. Then read Isaiah 40:25, 26.

1. A B C D E F H I J K L M N O P Q R S T U V W X Y Z

2. A B C D E F G H I J K L M N P Q R S T U V W X Y Z

3. A B C E F G H I J K L M N O P Q R S T U V W X Y Z

4. A B C D E F G I J K L M N O P Q R S T U V W X Y Z

5. B C D E F G H I J K L M N O P Q R S T U V W X Y Z

6. A B C D E F G H I J K L M N O P Q R T U V W X Y Z

7. A B C D E F G H I J K L M O P Q R S T U V W X Y Z

8. A B C D E F G H I J K L M N P Q R S T U V W X Y Z

9. A B C D F G H I J K L M N O P Q R S T U V W X Y Z

10. A B C D E F G H I J K L M N O P R S T U V W X Y Z

11. A B C D E F G H I J K L M N O P Q R S T V W X Y Z

12. B C D E F G H I J K L M N O P Q R S T U V W X Y Z

13. A B C D E F G H I J K M N O P Q R S T U V W X Y Z

__ __ __ __   __ __ __ __ __ __   __ __ __ __ __!

Through the Bible Puzzles, © 2001 by Standard Publishing • Permission granted to photocopy for classroom use only.

The Prophet

A prophet foretold the coming of a suffering servant of God, one who would bear the sins of many and suffer for their salvation. The suffering servant the prophet spoke of was Jesus. Do you know the name of the prophet? Trace the path through the maze. Then color in the path and you'll find the answer.

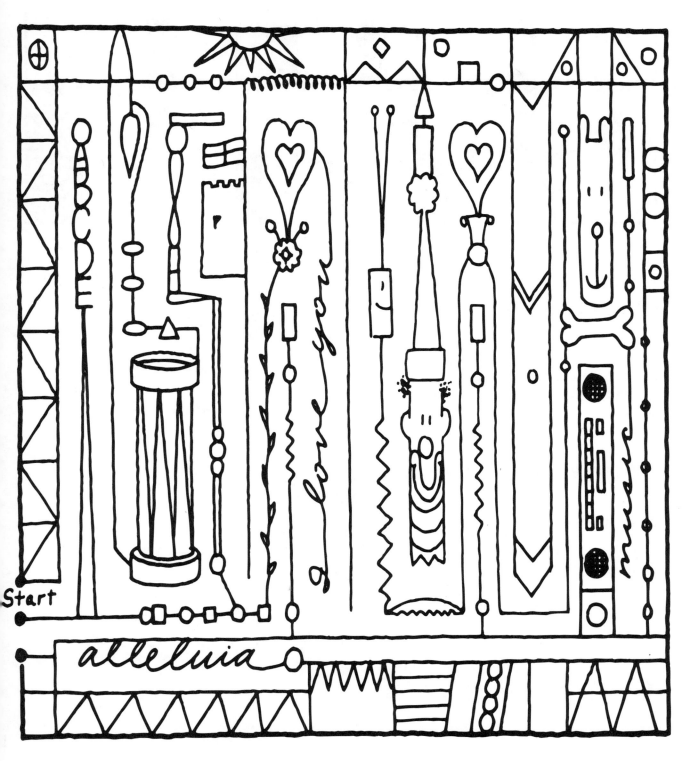

Taking Shape

Jeremiah was reminded that God is the Creator who shapes each person in his image. The Lord used a special example to help Jeremiah understand. To see what the Lord said, find the answers to the clues. Copy the letters of your answers into the puzzle boxes. Then read Jeremiah 18:1-6.

1	2	3	4		5	6	7	8		9	10		11	12	13		14	15	16	17
	18	19		20	21	22		23	24	25	26	27	28		,		29	30		
31	32	33		34	35	36		37	38		39	40		41	42	43	44			
																	∎			

1. One who paints or draws— $\overline{7}$ $\overline{32}$ $\overline{26}$ $\overline{2}$ $\overline{29}$ $\overline{11}$

2. Something around a picture— $\overline{19}$ $\overline{28}$ $\overline{15}$ $\overline{39}$ $\overline{27}$

3. Item at the end of a fishing line— $\overline{12}$ $\overline{18}$ $\overline{30}$ $\overline{3}$

4. Writing instrument— $\overline{23}$ $\overline{13}$ $\overline{10}$

5. Contraction for you + would— $\overline{8}$ $\overline{24}$ $\overline{36}$ $\overline{44}$

6. Easter flower— $\overline{1}$ $\overline{37}$ $\overline{6}$ $\overline{40}$

7. What bees make— $\overline{14}$ $\overline{35}$ $\overline{43}$ $\overline{22}$ $\overline{34}$

8. A good one is on your shoulders— $\overline{21}$ $\overline{4}$ $\overline{31}$ $\overline{17}$

9. Camping need— $\overline{20}$ $\overline{33}$ $\overline{38}$ $\overline{25}$

10. Fancy dishes or a country— $\overline{5}$ $\overline{41}$ $\overline{9}$ $\overline{16}$ $\overline{42}$

Through the Bible Puzzles, © 2001 by Standard Publishing • Permission granted to photocopy for classroom use only.

Cistern Escape

The Israelites threw Jeremiah into a cistern. How did he get out? Find the book of Jeremiah in your Bible and answer the questions below. Then take the letters from the circles and write them in the rocks. Read Jeremiah 38:3-10.

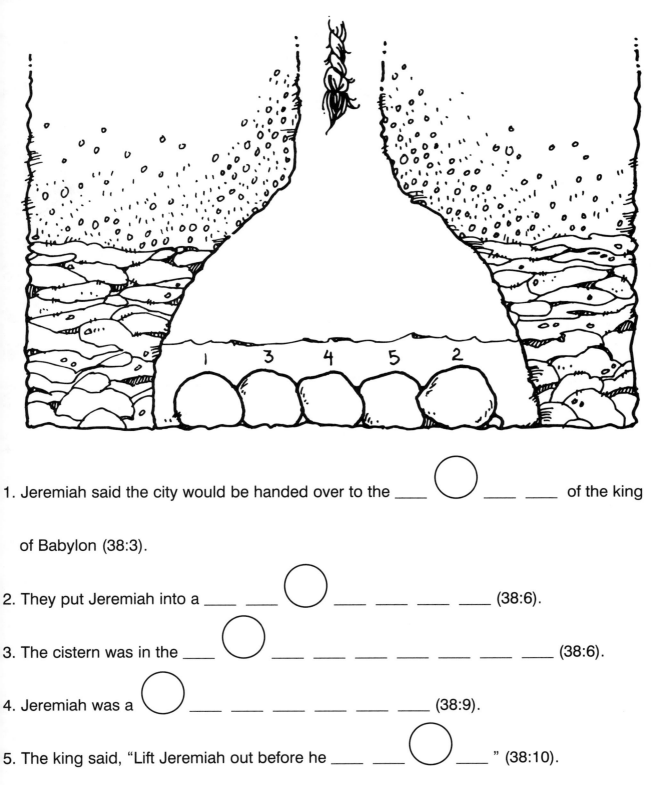

1. Jeremiah said the city would be handed over to the ___ ◯ ___ ___ of the king

of Babylon (38:3).

2. They put Jeremiah into a ___ ___ ◯ ___ ___ ___ ___ (38:6).

3. The cistern was in the ___ ◯ ___ ___ ___ ___ ___ ___ ___ (38:6).

4. Jeremiah was a ◯ ___ ___ ___ ___ ___ ___ (38:9).

5. The king said, "Lift Jeremiah out before he ___ ___ ◯ ___ " (38:10).

Through the Bible Puzzles, © 2001 by Standard Publishing • Permission granted to photocopy for classroom use only.

Captured!

Read Jeremiah 39:1-12 and 40:1-4. Number the events in order 1–9. Then fill in the blanks below by copying in order the letter from the top of each link to find out why Jerusalem fell.

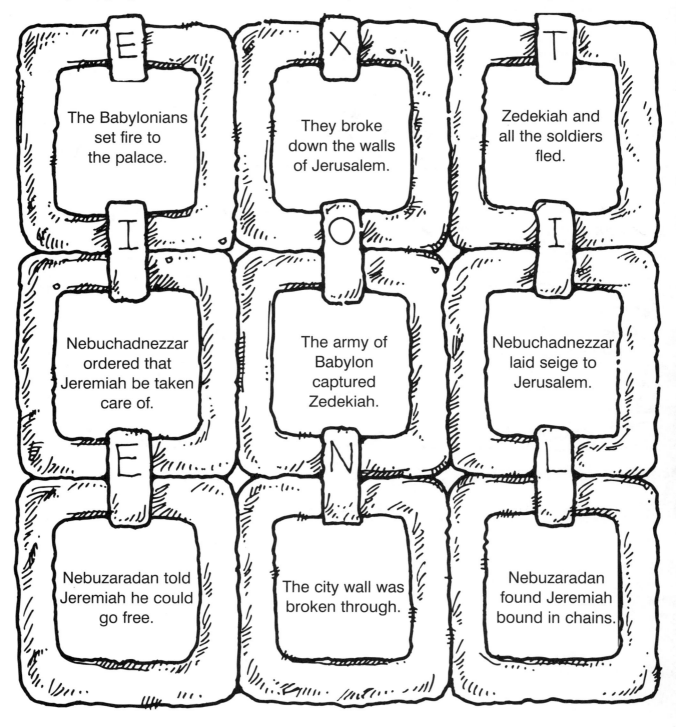

The Babylonians set fire to the palace.

They broke down the walls of Jerusalem.

Zedekiah and all the soldiers fled.

Nebuchadnezzar ordered that Jeremiah be taken care of.

The army of Babylon captured Zedekiah.

Nebuchadnezzar laid seige to Jerusalem.

Nebuzaradan told Jeremiah he could go free.

The city wall was broken through.

Nebuzaradan found Jeremiah bound in chains.

The captives from Jerusalem and Judah were carried ____ ____ ____ ____

____ ____ ____ ____ ____ to Babylon. Jeremiah 40:1

  Through the Bible Puzzles, © 2001 by Standard Publishing • Permission granted to photocopy for classroom use only.

Follow Directions

Zedekiah did not follow the Lord's directions. (See Jeremiah 52:1-11.) Carefully follow these directions.

1. Cross out all words beginning with the letter Q.

2. Cross out all names of buildings.

3. Cross out all words with 12 or more letters.

4. Cross out all names of bodies of water.

5. Cross out all names of flowers.

Now read the leftover words from left to right in order to flind out what happened when Zedekiah disobeyed God's laws.

ZEDEKIAH	QUEEN	PALACE	ROSE
SCHOOL	BECAME	KING	NEBUCHADNEZZAR
AND	TULIP	DID	EVIL.
DAISY	HE	TURNED	DAFFODIL
AWAY	FROM	HOUSE	QUIT
CREEK	QUIET	LAKE	GOD.
THE	ZINNIA	BABYLONIAN	PETUNIA
ARMY	QUIZ	SURROUNDED	SEA
FACTORY	THE	QUILT	CITY.
PEOPLE	STARVED.	SOON	THE
OCEAN	RIVER	ARMY	BROKE
IN	MARIGOLD	AND	OFFICE
BURNED	QUICK	LILY	EVERYTHING.

Through the Bible Puzzles, © 2001 by Standard Publishing • Permission granted to photocopy for classroom use only.

The Lord's Promise

Read Ezekiel 36:27. Use a pencil to trace a path through the maze. Follow the letters of the words in this verse.

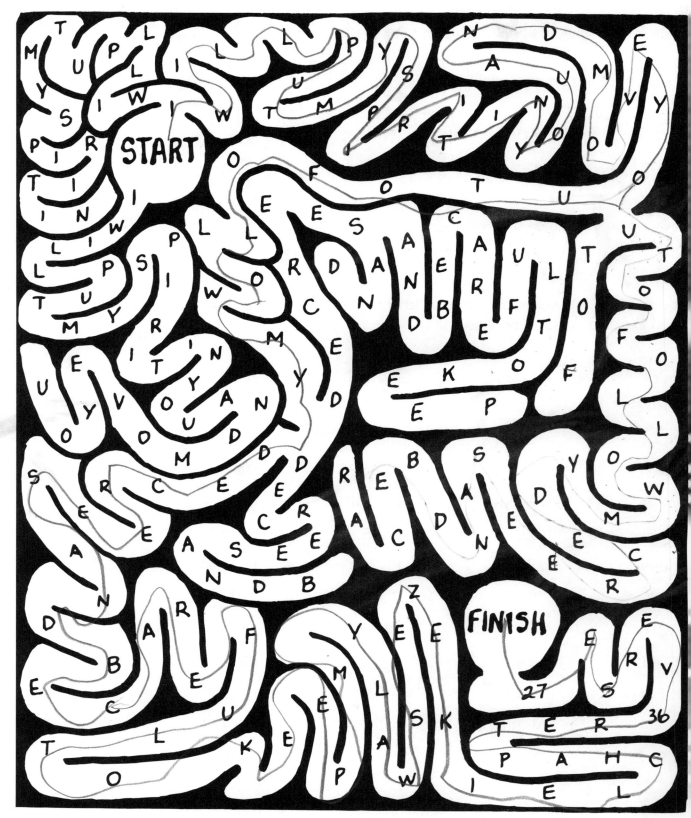

Through the Bible Puzzles, © 2001 by Standard Publishing • Permission granted to photocopy for classroom use only.

What's on the Menu?

In Daniel 1, Daniel and his friends chose their own meals. Follow the paths from the men on the left to the plates on the right. Write the letters in the blanks at the bottom in the order the men appear.

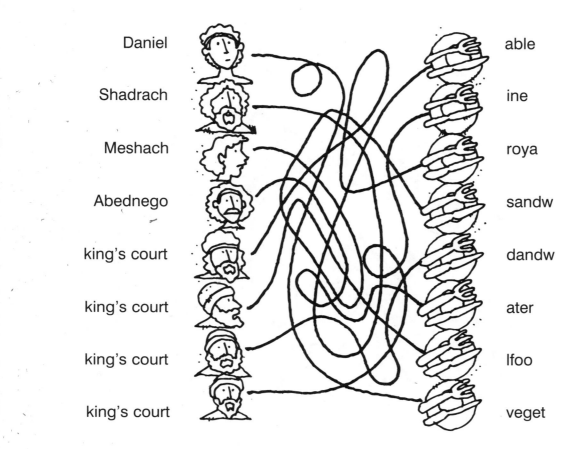

Daniel, Shadrach, Meshach, and Abednego ate

___ ___ ___ ___ ___ ___ ___ ___ ___ ___

___ ___ ___ ___ ___ ___ ___ .

The men from the king's court ate

___ ___ ___ ___ ___ ___

___ ___ ___ ___ ___ ___ .

God Protects His Faithful

King Nebuchadnezzar declared that everyone had to worship a gold statue instead of God. Some of the Jews disobeyed this command, and this made the king very angry. He ordered these people thrown into a blazing furnace. To find out what happened, begin with the letter S by the star. Use a light color to color in every other letter on the path around the flames. Write the colored letters, then the uncolored ones in the blanks below. (See Daniel 3.)

_ _ _ _ _ _ _ _ , _ _ _ _ _ _ _ , _ _ _

_ _ _ _ _ _ _ _ _ _ _ _ _ _

_ _ _ _ _ _ _ _ _ _ _ _

_ _ _ _ _ _ _ _ _ _ _ _

_ _ _ _ _ _ _ _ _ _ _ _ .

Through the Bible Puzzles, © 2001 by Standard Publishing • Permission granted to photocopy for classroom use only.

The King Learns a Lesson

Read Daniel 4:30-37. Read each sentence below. If the sentence is true, color the circle in the TRUE column. If the sentence is not true, color the circle in the FALSE column. Copy the colored letters first, then the uncolored ones onto the blanks below to find a message.

		TRUE	FALSE
1.	God said Nebuchadnezzar would lose his royal authority (v. 31).	O	L
2.	The king was driven away from the people (v. 33).	N	L
3.	He had to eat birds and fish (v. 33).	P	L
4.	His nails grew like bird claws (v. 33).	Y	O
5.	At the end of the time, he looked up to heaven (v. 34).	G	W
6.	He refused to honor and glorify God (v. 34).	E	O
7.	His honor as king was restored (v. 36).	D	R
8.	His advisors took over his throne (v. 36).	F	I
9.	He became greater than before (v. 36).	S	U
10.	He said that God's ways were not just (v. 37).	L	A

____ ____ ____ ____   ____ ____ ____ ____   ____ ____

____ ____ ____   ____ ____ ____ ____ ____ ____ ____ ____ ____ ____ .

Handwriting on the Wall

King Belshazzar gave a party. He and his guests drank wine and praised false gods. Suddenly a hand appeared and wrote a message on the wall. The words below tell what the message meant. Use the numbered letters to fill in the puzzle. The finished puzzle will tell you what happened to King Belshazzar. (See Daniel 5.)

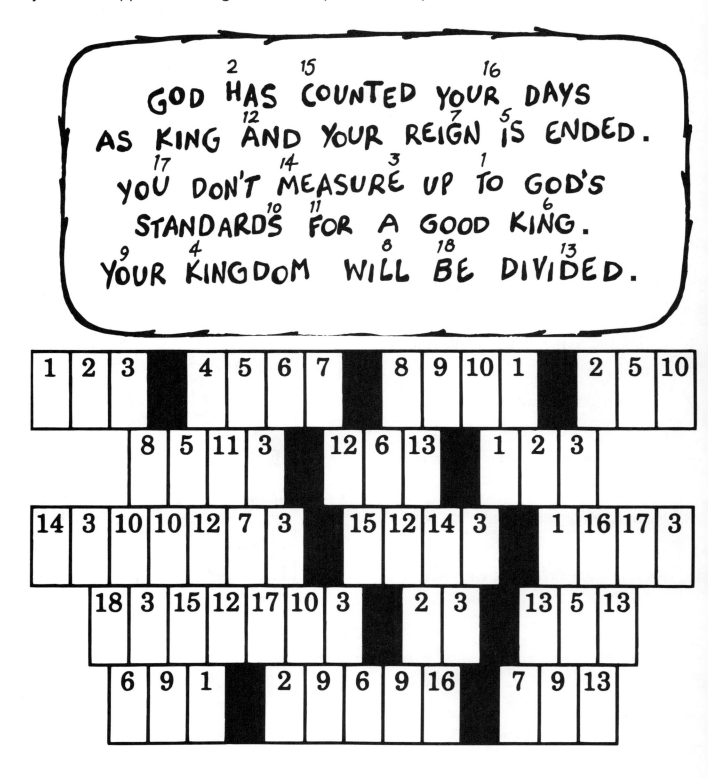

GOD HAS COUNTED YOUR DAYS
AS KING AND YOUR REIGN IS ENDED.
YOU DON'T MEASURE UP TO GOD'S
STANDARDS FOR A GOOD KING.
YOUR KINGDOM WILL BE DIVIDED.

Through the Bible Puzzles, © 2001 by Standard Publishing • Permission granted to photocopy for classroom use only.

Lion Tamer

Using a ruler, draw a line from the letter under the lion on the top row to the left ear of the matching lion on the bottom row. Each line will go through letters in the middle of the page. Copy the letters in order at the bottom of the page. Read Daniel 6 to learn about Daniel in the lion's den.

G s g   s   t   e   o   m   t

,

___ ___ ___ ___ ___ ___

___ ___ ___   ___ ___

,

___ ___ ___ ___ ___ ___ ___ ___ ___

A Straight Wall

A plumb line is used to help build a straight wall. Make this wall tall and straight by finding the words with A in them and fitting them in the bricks. First read Amos 1:1 and 7:7-16.

1.   _____ was the shepherd who became a prophet (1:1).

2.   He was a prophet when _____ was king of Judah (1:1).

3.   He was a prophet when Jeroboam son of Jehoash was king

     of _____ (1:1).

4.   Amos was among the shepherds of _____ (1:1).

5.   Amos was a prophet two _____ before the earthquake (1:1).

6.   The Lord was standing by a wall with a plumb line in his _____ (7:7).

7.   The _____ of Israel will be ruined (7:9).

8.   The Lord will rise against the house of_____ with a sword (7:9).

9.   _____ was the priest of Bethel (7:10).

10. This priest thought Amos was raising a _____ against

     Jeroboam (7:10).

11. Amaziah told Amos to get out and go back to the land of _____ (7:12).

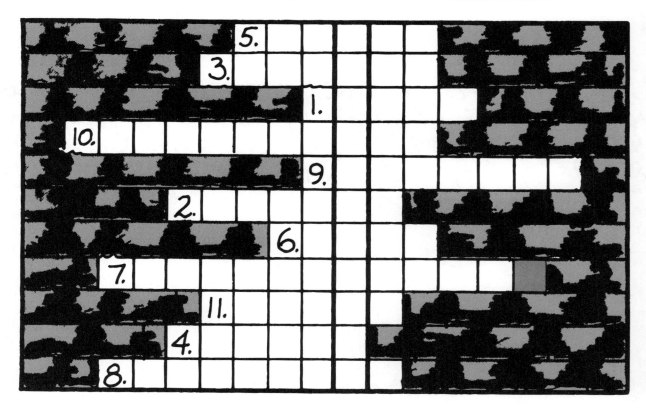

Through the Bible Puzzles, © 2001 by Standard Publishing • Permission granted to photocopy for classroom use only.

Crazy Clues

Choose a letter of the alphabet for each crazy clue below. Then fill in the same letter in all the boxes with the same number. (The letter for clue 1 goes in all the boxes with a 1.) When all the letters are filled in, read what the people in Haggai 1:2-14 did.

1. If you add this letter to *kit*, you have something you can fly with a string.

2. This letter is in both *tea* and *fist*.

3. The sound a cat makes has this letter in it. So does the sound an owl makes and the sound a cow makes.

4. If you add this letter to *sake*, you have something that's cool and frosty (and chocolate, vanilla, or strawberry).

5. This letter plus *nt* makes a small, crawling creature. This letter plus *rk* makes a big boat.

6. This letter sometimes sounds like *eeeee*. It's a crazy letter. It's also the next-to-last letter of the alphabet.

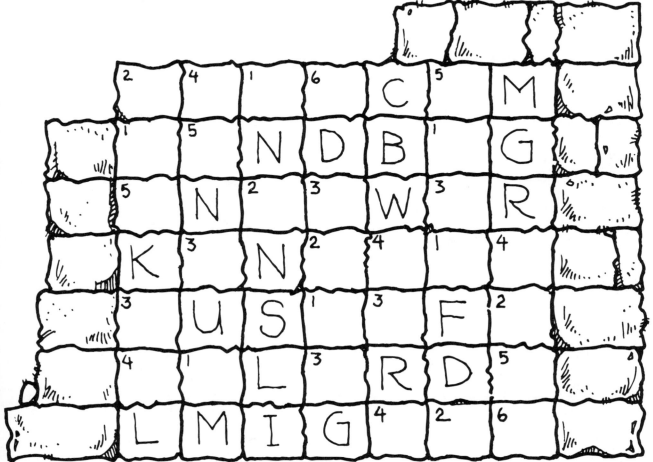

Give and Receive

Use these picture and letter clues to find the message from Malachi 3:8-12.

_ _ _ _ _ _   _ _ _ _ _ _

_ _ _   _ _ _ _ _ _ _ _

_ _ _ _ _   _ _ _ _

_ _ _ _ _   _ _ _

_ _ _ _ _ _ _

 Through the Bible Puzzles, © 2001 by Standard Publishing • Permission granted to photocopy for classroom use only.

The Genealogy of Jesus

Read Matthew 1:1-17. Write the son's name beside his father. Then write the letters that match the symbols on the lines below. Number the fathers in historical order.

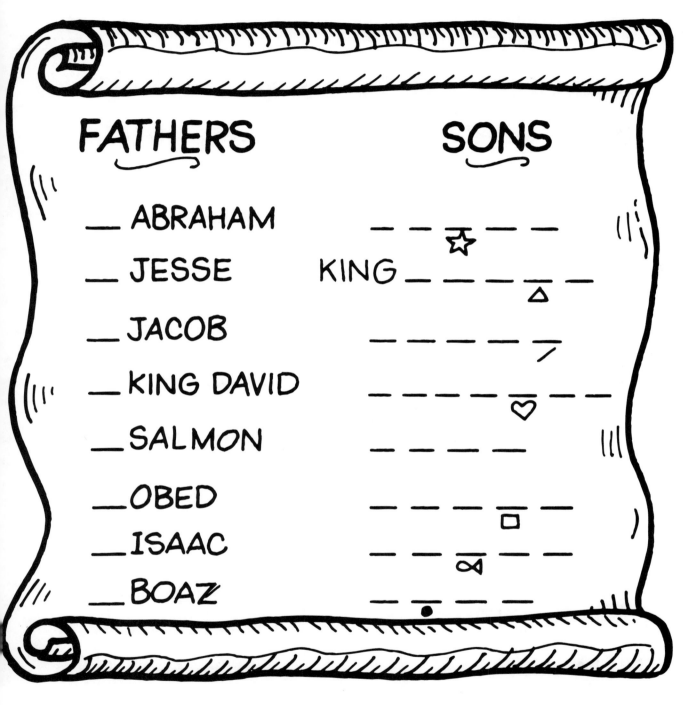

FATHERS

__ ABRAHAM

__ JESSE

__ JACOB

__ KING DAVID

__ SALMON

__ OBED

__ ISAAC

__ BOAZ

SONS

There were **30 + 12** generations from

___ ___ R ___ ___ ___ ___ ___ TO ___ ___ R ___ ___ T.

A Gift for Me?

Finish the sentence from Matthew 1:21 by going through the maze. Pick up the letters as you go and put them on the lines below. There is only one correct path. When completed, you will know why God gave us this gift.

You are to give him the name _____

_____

_____

    Through the Bible Puzzles, © 2001 by Standard Publishing • Permission granted to photocopy for classroom use only.

Come and Worship!

Read Matthew 2:1-11 which tells the story of the wise men. Then fill in the puzzle using the clues given. The shaded squares will spell the name of an important city.

1. When they found the child, they _____ down (v. 11).

2. Magi from the _____ came to Jerusalem (v. 1).

3. "We saw his _____" (v. 2).

4. Herod asked them where the _____ was to be born (v. 4).

5. They presented him with gifts of _____ (v. 11).

6. The child's name was _____ (v. 1).

7. The child was born during the time of King _____ (v. 1).

8. Jesus was born in a town in _____ (v. 1).

9. _____ came from the east to Jerusalem (v. 1).

Star Search

Draw a line from the first part of each word on the top line to the last part of the word in the second line. Start and end your lines on the dots. The words are names of people and places in Matthew 2:1, 2, 11-23. After you have connected all the names, write the letters crossed by the lines in order from left to right in the blanks at the bottom of the page. You will find out what the Magi did when they saw Jesus.

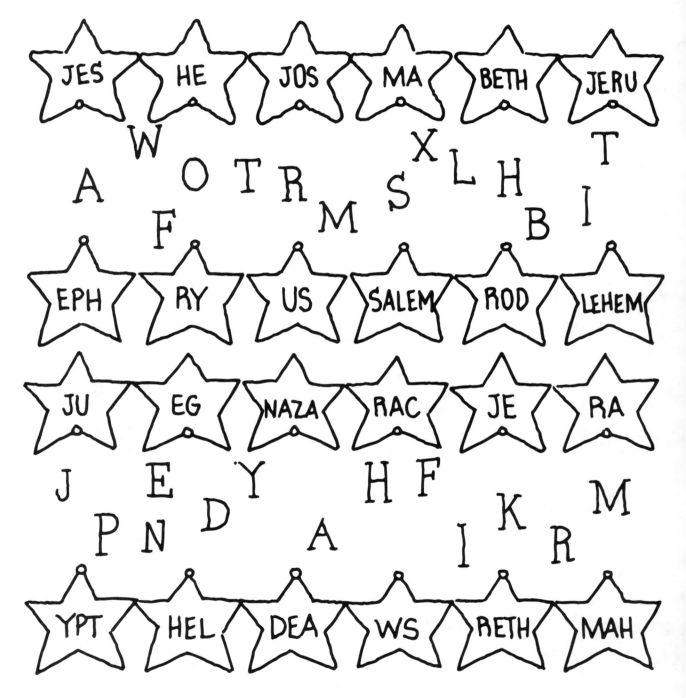

___ ___ ___ ___ ___ ___ ___ ___ ___ ___ ___ ___ ___ ___ ___ ___ ___ ___ ___!

 Through the Bible Puzzles, © 2001 by Standard Publishing • Permission granted to photocopy for classroom use only.

Jesus Is Baptized

Matthew 3:13-17 tells us of the baptism of Jesus. But what happened when Jesus was baptized? Use the code to find the answer.

The Spirit

Read Matthew 3:16, 17. Follow the stringed letters and write them in order on the lines below. Then break the letters into words.

GOD SAID,"_____

_____

_____." MATTHEW 3:17

 Through the Bible Puzzles, © 2001 by Standard Publishing • Permission granted to photocopy for classroom use only.

Yield Not to Temptation

Follow the traffic signs to find a message that helped Jesus steer away from the devil. Each sign stands for a letter. Learn which letter from the partly decoded message below. Read Matthew 4:1-11 for help. Then decode the message.

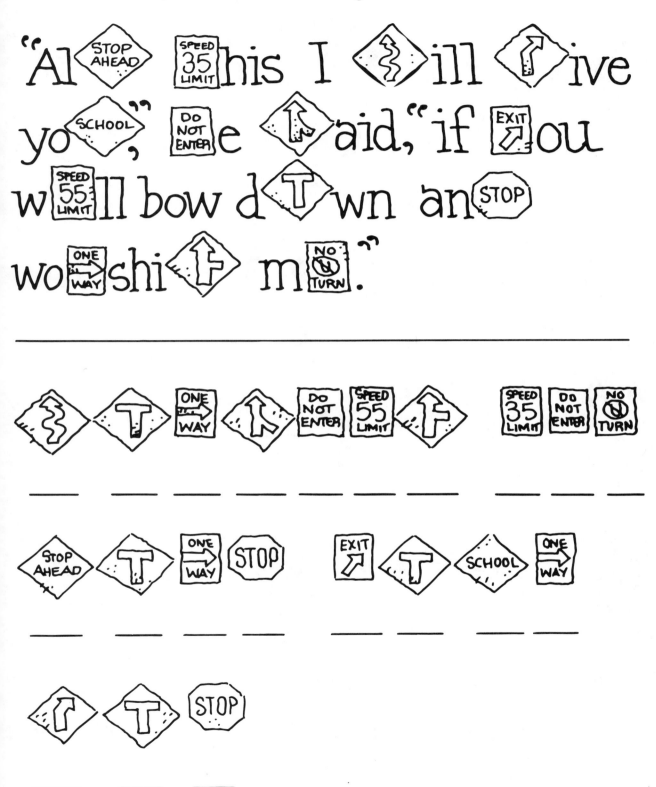

Calling Followers

Read Matthew 4:18-22; 9:9; Mark 3:13-19. Unscramble the names on the lines provided. Then finish the sentence with the letters that you figured out really belong with symbols.

P E̤ E T R   **M** T T W E A H (△)

J S M E A (○)   **T** M O H S A (□)

J N O H   **J** S E M A (◇)

A D W R N E   **S** M O T N

J D A U S   **T** H A D E U S D A

B A R T H M E W O L O (☆)(○)   **P** L T T P H (▽)(♡)

These men were Jesus'

☆	♡	□	○	△	▽	◇	◉

102 Through the Bible Puzzles, © 2001 by Standard Publishing • Permission granted to photocopy for classroom use only.

Through the Bible Puzzles, © 2001 by Standard Publishing • Permission granted to photocopy for classroom use only.

Who Is Blessed?

Read Matthew 5:1-12. Then color in only the spaces below that name the people who Jesus said would be blessed. You will find out where Jesus was teaching.

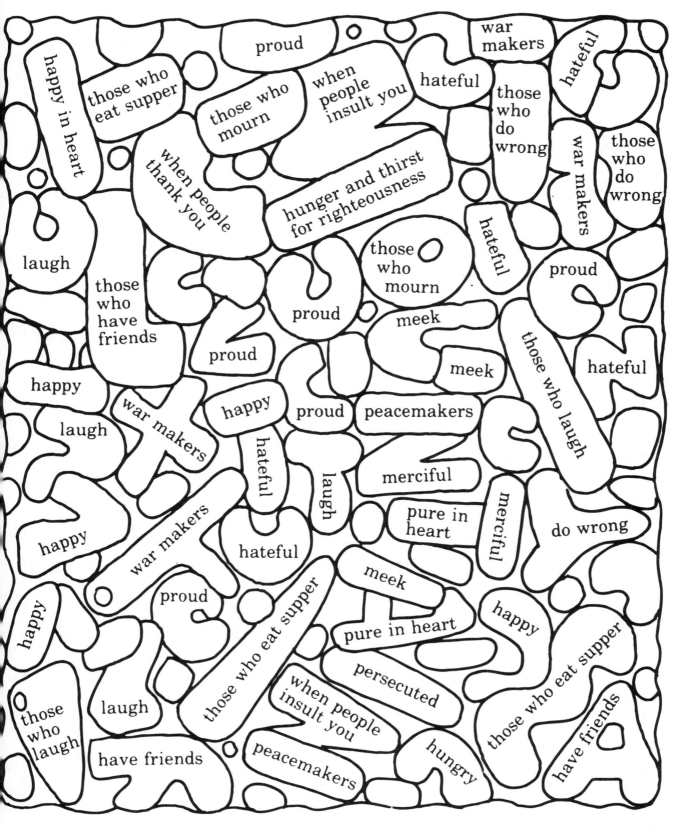

Through the Bible Puzzles, © 2001 by Standard Publishing • Permission granted to photocopy for classroom use only.

What Am I?

Read the story below by changing its letters and pictures into words. Then read
Matthew 5:13-16.

   Through the Bible Puzzles, © 2001 by Standard Publishing • Permission granted to photocopy for classroom use only.

A Wise Builder

People use many different things to build their houses. Jesus talked about how to build wisely or foolishly. Choose the right materials to solve the code that tells you who is a wise builder. Read Matthew 7:24-29 to find out more.

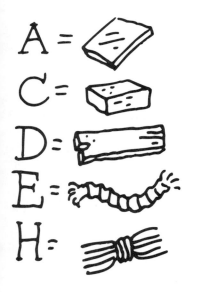
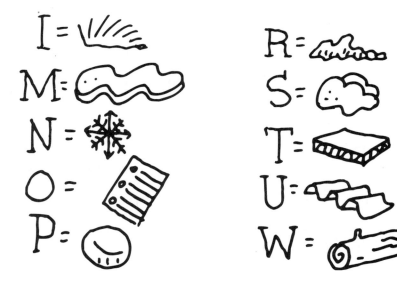

A wise builder is one who . . .

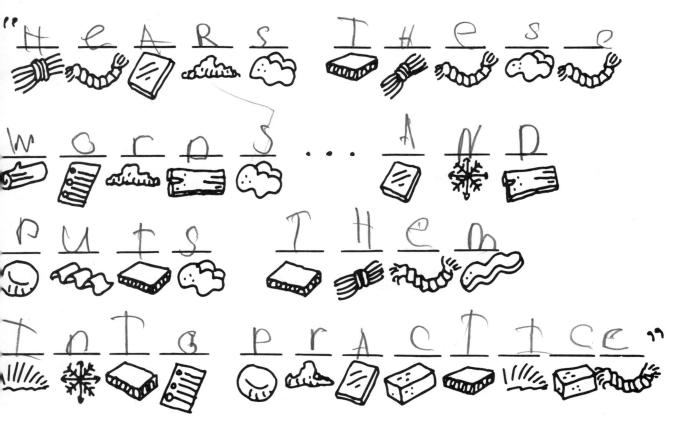

"HEARS THESE

WORDS . . . AND

PUTS THEM

INTO PRACTICE"

Twelve Men

Use the letters of the word *disciples* to place the names of nine of the twelve disciples in the grid below. You will find them mentioned in Matthew 10:2-4 and John 1:35-45.

1.   Simon Peter's brother

2.   The Zealot

3.   Listed just before the tax collector

4.   The betrayer

5.   Andrew's brother

6.   Listed before Bartholomew

7.   Listed after Philip in Matthew; John calls him Nathanael

8.   Son of Alphaeus

9.   Named before Simon, he is also known as Judas

Now, can you name the other three?

_____ , _____ , and _____ .

Through the Bible Puzzles, © 2001 by Standard Publishing • Permission granted to photocopy for classroom use only.

Find the Treasure

Find the missing words of Matthew 13:44-46 hidden in and on the treasure chest. A number is included with each word. Place the word in the blank with the same number.

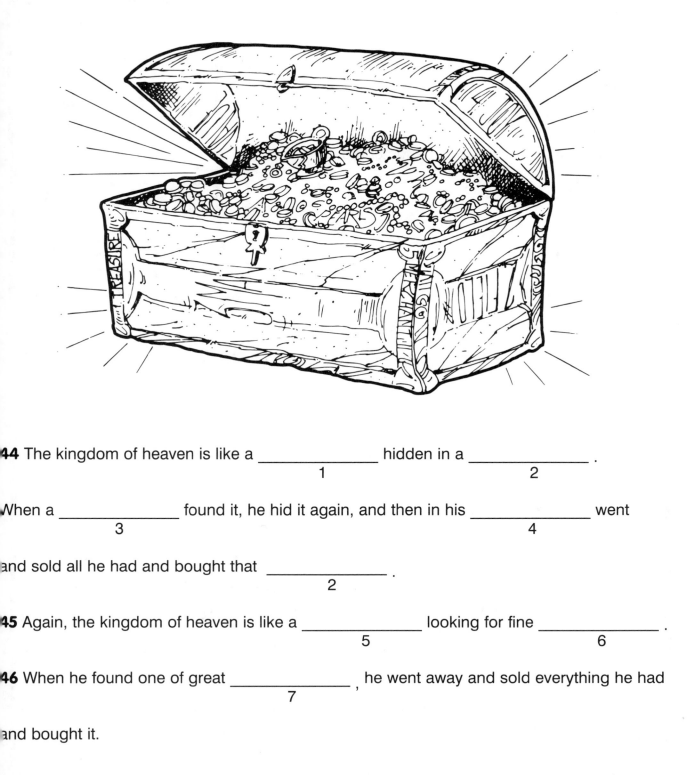

44 The kingdom of heaven is like a _____ hidden in a _____ .
                                        1   2

When a _____ found it, he hid it again, and then in his _____ went
           3   4

and sold all he had and bought that _____ .
                                         2

45 Again, the kingdom of heaven is like a _____ looking for fine _____ .
                                                 5   6

46 When he found one of great _____ , he went away and sold everything he had
                                       7

and bought it.

Through the Bible Puzzles, © 2001 by Standard Publishing • Permission granted to photocopy for classroom use only.

Cross It Out

Read Matthew 14:1-12. Then follow the directions below.

1.   Cross out one brother.

2.   Cross out one wife.

3.   Cross out one girl.

4.   Cross out two words for John.

5.   Cross out three things the daughter did.

6.   Cross out one word for jail.

7.   Cross out three groups of people.

8.   Cross out a word telling how John was killed.

9.   Cross out two titles for Herod.

10.   Now circle the words from Exodus 20:14.

11.   The words that are left tell how Herod reacted to John's message from God

      (Matthew 14:5).

PHILIP	YOU	HEROD	DAUGHTER	GUSTS
SHALL	WANTED	PROPHET	PLEASED	ATTENDANTS
BEHEADED	KING	NOT	TO	CARRIED
DISCIPLES	DANCED	BAPTIST	KILL	COMMIT
HERODIAS	ADULTERY	JOHN	TETRARCH	PRISON

 Through the Bible Puzzles, © 2001 by Standard Publishing • Permission granted to photocopy for classroom use only.

Jesus Walked on Water

Read Matthew 14:22-33. Unscramble the large letters to find a name. Then write the large letters in the correct order in the top of the empty box. Copy the columns under each bold letter in the correct order. Now read from left to right to find the answer from Matthew 14:33.

E	U	J	S	S
those	were	Then	who	in
boat	him	the	worshiped	saying
you	the	Truly	are	Son
God	❁	of	❁	❁

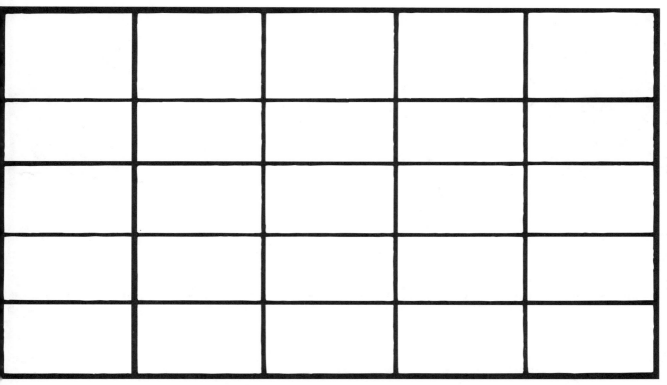

Peter's Confession Hourglass

Read Matthew 16:13-17. Write the missing words from the story on the lines by the correct number.

When **12** came to the **4** of Caesarea **2**, he asked his **1**, "**7 8** people say the Son of Man **9**?" They replied, "**6** say **11** the **14**; others say Elijah; and still others, **15** or one of the prophets." "But what about **10**?" he asked. "Who do you say I am?" Simon Peter answered, "You are the **13**, the Son of the **16**."Jesus replied, "**3** are you, Simon son of **5**, for this was not revealed to you by man, but by my Father in heaven."

1. _____ _____ _____ _____ _____ _____ _____

2. _____ _____ _____ _____ _____ _____

3. _____ _____ _____ _____ _____

4. _____ _____ _____ _____ _____

5. _____ _____ _____ _____

6. _____ _____ _____ _____

7. _____ _____ _____

8. _____ _____

9. _____ _____

10. _____ _____ _____

11. _____ _____ _____ _____

12. _____ _____ _____ _____ _____

13. _____ _____ _____ _____ _____ _____

14. _____ _____ _____ _____ _____ _____

15. _____ _____ _____ _____ _____ _____

16. _____ _____ _____ _____ _____ _____ _____

Through the Bible Puzzles, © 2001 by Standard Publishing • Permission granted to photocopy for classroom use only.

Forgive

Peter asked Jesus if he should forgive his brother seven times. What was Jesus' answer? Put the words in the shapes in the matching shapes in the heart. Then read Matthew 18:21-35 to find out more about forgiveness.

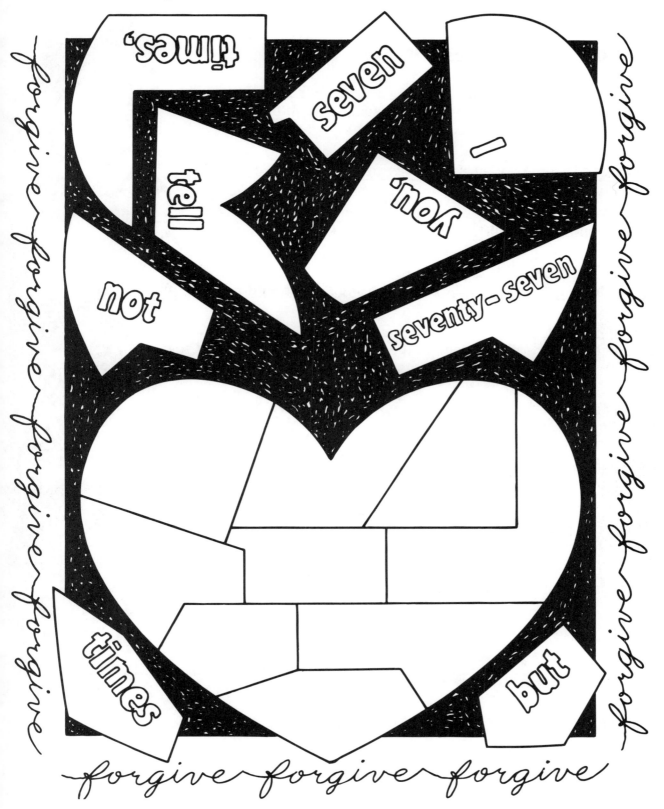

Two Sons

Read Matthew 21:28-32 (ICB) and check the right answers. Copy the letter from each correct box onto the first line. Then copy the letters from the wrong answer boxes onto the second line.

There was a man who had **one**[E] **two**[C] sons.

He went to the **first**[H] **second**[N] son and said, "**Daughter**[T] **Son**[A],

go and **work**[N] **play**[E] today in my **vineyard**[G] **barn**[R]."

The son answered, "I **will**[T] **will not**[E] go."

But later the **son**[A] **daughter**[H] decided he **should**[N] **should not**[E] go, and he went.

Then the **mother**[K] **father**[D] went to the other **son**[B] **daughter**[I] and said,

"Son, go and **work**[E] **play**[N] today in my **vineyard**[L] **barn**[G]."

The son answered, **No**[D] **Yes**[I], sir, I **will**[E] **will not**[O] go and work."

But he did not go. Which of the **two**[V] **three**[M] sons obeyed his father?

The priests and leaders answered, "The **first**[E] **second** son."

— — — — — — — — — — — — — — — —

— — — — — — — — — — — — — — — —

Through the Bible Puzzles, © 2001 by Standard Publishing • Permission granted to photocopy for classroom use only.

When Will Jesus Come?

Follow the lines from the lanterns to the blank spaces and put the letters that are in the lanterns on the spaces. You will find out what we know about when Jesus will return. Read Matthew 25:1-13 to find out more.

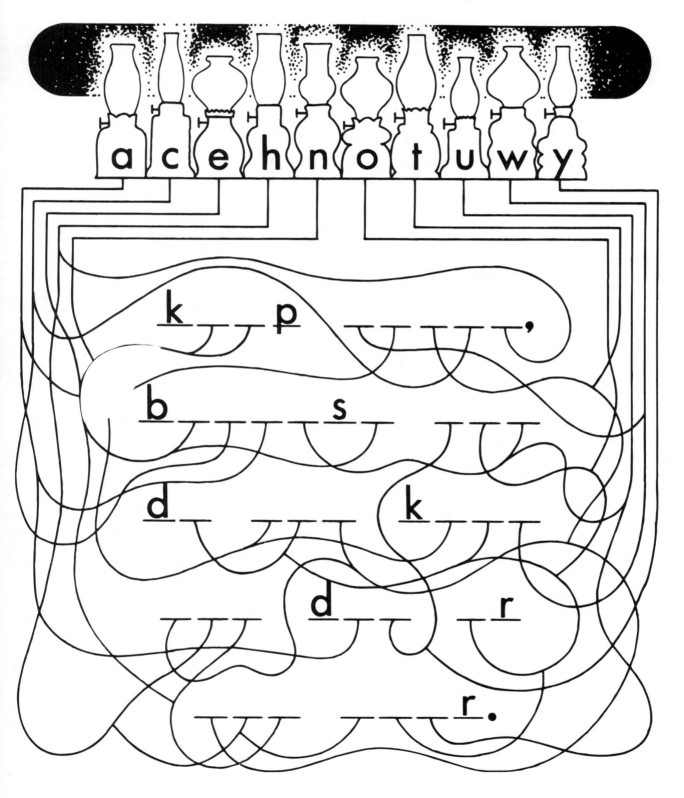

One Talent

1. Subtract box **C** from box **F**. Place the answer in workbox **A**.

2. Subtract box **D** from box **A**. Place the answer in workbox **B**.

3. Add boxes **C** and **D**. Place the total in workbox **C**.

4. Add boxes **E** and **F**. Place the total in workbox **D**.

5. Subtract box **D** from box **E**. Place the answer in workbox **E**.

6. Add boxes **C**, **D**, and **F**. Place the total in workbox **F**.

7. Subtract box **A** from box **G**. Place the answer in workbox **G**.

8. Add boxes **B** and **F**. Place the total in workbox **H**.

Boxes

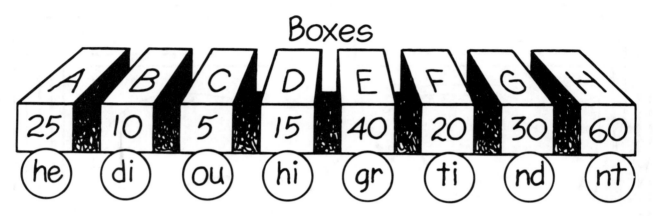

In the circles below each workbox, write the letters that appear below the same number at the top of the page. Read Matthew 25:24-30 to find out more.

Workboxes

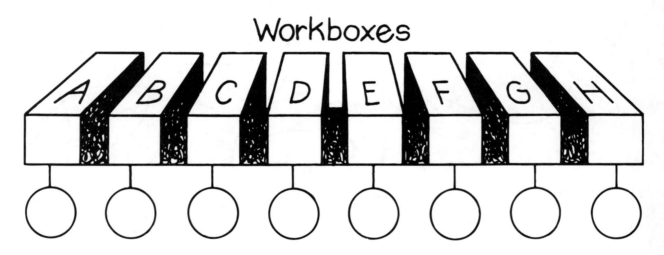

What did the servant with one talent do with his money?

 Through the Bible Puzzles, © 2001 by Standard Publishing • Permission granted to photocopy for classroom use only.

What's the Question?

Read Matthew 25:31-46 and then color in the coded squares to read the question from the Scripture. Some of the squares have been filled in for you.

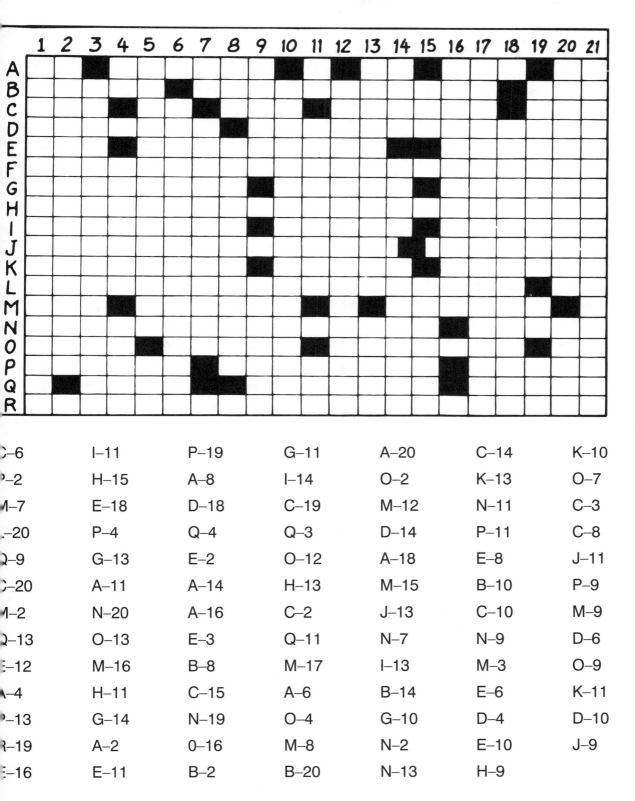

C–6	I–11	P–19	G–11	A–20	C–14	K–10
P–2	H–15	A–8	I–14	O–2	K–13	O–7
M–7	E–18	D–18	C–19	M–12	N–11	C–3
–20	P–4	Q–4	Q–3	D–14	P–11	C–8
Q–9	G–13	E–2	O–12	A–18	E–8	J–11
C–20	A–11	A–14	H–13	M–15	B–10	P–9
M–2	N–20	A–16	C–2	J–13	C–10	M–9
Q–13	O–13	E–3	Q–11	N–7	N–9	D–6
E–12	M–16	B–8	M–17	I–13	M–3	O–9
A–4	H–11	C–15	A–6	B–14	E–6	K–11
P–13	G–14	N–19	O–4	G–10	D–4	D–10
R–19	A–2	0–16	M–8	N–2	E–10	J–9
E–16	E–11	B–2	B–20	N–13	H–9	

See the Stone?

Read Matthew 28:1-10. A message from Matthew 28:1-10 is hidden in the stones of this puzzle. Color all the spaces where the stones overlap, then read the uncolored words to find the message.

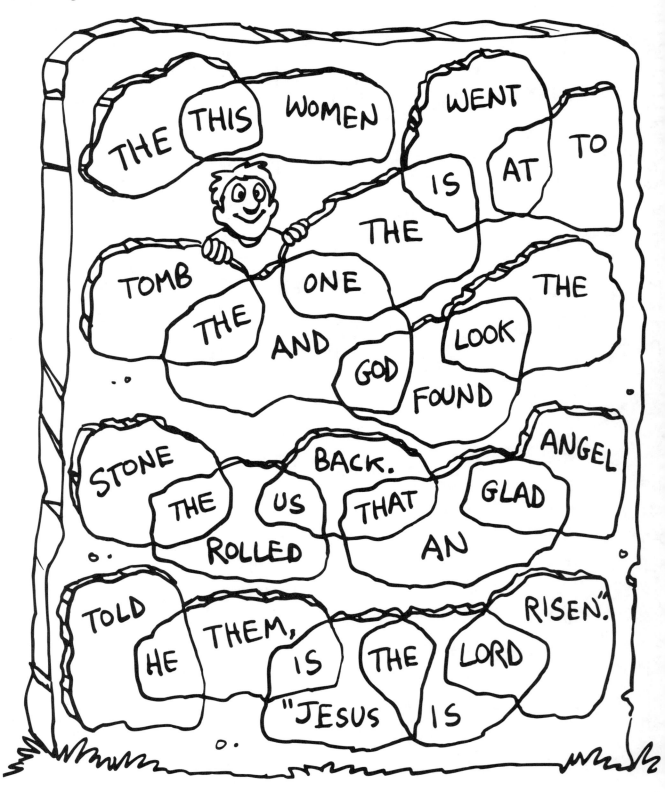

 Through the Bible Puzzles, © 2001 by Standard Publishing • Permission granted to photocopy for classroom use only.

A Final Message

Read Matthew 28:16-20 for help. What did Jesus say to his disciples before he returned to Heaven? To find out, turn the letters below into words by adding vowels.

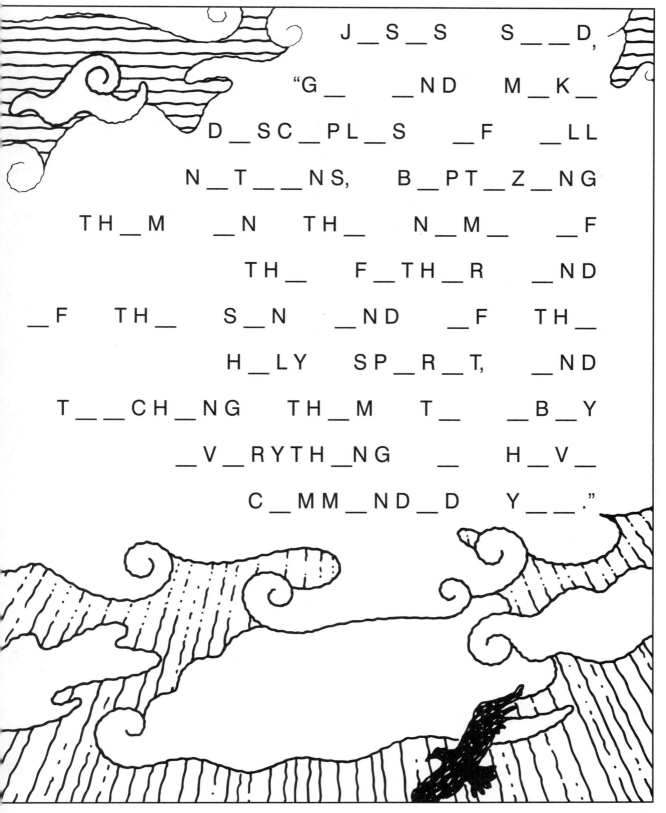

J _ S _ S   S _ _ D,

"G _   _ ND   M _ K _

D _ SC _ PL _ S   _ F   _ LL

N _ T _ _ NS,   B _ PT _ Z _ NG

TH _ M   _ N   TH _   N _ M _   _ F

TH _   F _ TH _ R   _ ND

_ F   TH _   S _ N   _ ND   _ F   TH _

H _ LY   SP _ R _ T,   _ ND

T _ _ CH _ NG   TH _ M   T _   _ B _ Y

_ V _ RYTH _ NG   _   H _ V _

C _ MM _ ND _ D   Y _ _ ."

Through the Bible Puzzles, © 2001 by Standard Publishing • Permission granted to photocopy for classroom use only.

Forgiven!

What is the first thing Jesus said to the paralyzed man? To find out, go down the line of boxes below each number on the graph and find the colored squares. Do numbers 1 through 10 in order. Write the letters from beside the colored squares in order in the blanks of the message. Read Mark 2:1-12 to find out more.

" _____ , _____ _____ _____ _____ _____ ."

Why did Jesus tell the paralyzed man to get up, take up his mat, and go home? To find out, put each letter that has a symbol beside it on the line above the same symbol.

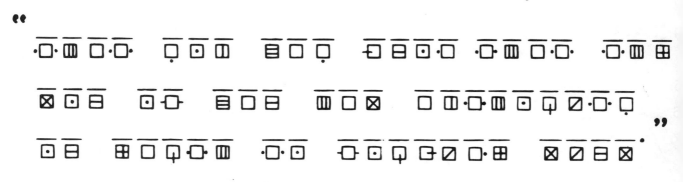

Through the Bible Puzzles, © 2001 by Standard Publishing • Permission granted to photocopy for classroom use only.

Healing of the Demon-Possessed Man

Read Mark 5:1-20. Then read each statement below and follow the directions. When completed, you will find something from the Scripture you just read.

1. If Jesus went to the Gerasenes, color the 2s black and the 9s yellow.

2. If a man who lived in the tombs had never been chained, color the 4s blue and the 3s green.

3. If the man's name was Larry, color the 8s red and the 5s black.

4. If the demons begged to be sent into a herd of pigs, color the 5s orange and the 6s black.

5. If the evil spirits came out of the man into the pigs, color the 4s black and the 7s green.

6. If there were about 200 pigs, color the 8s yellow and the 1s purple.

7. If the pigs drowned, color the 3s red and the 8s black.

8. If the people were afraid, color the 1s blue.

Through the Bible Puzzles, © 2001 by Standard Publishing • Permission granted to photocopy for classroom use only.

A Rich Man's Mistake

Jesus told a rich young man to sell everything he had and follow him. What did the rich man do? Work these math problems to learn the code. Then fill in the blanks below to find out. Read Mark 10:17-22 to check your answer.

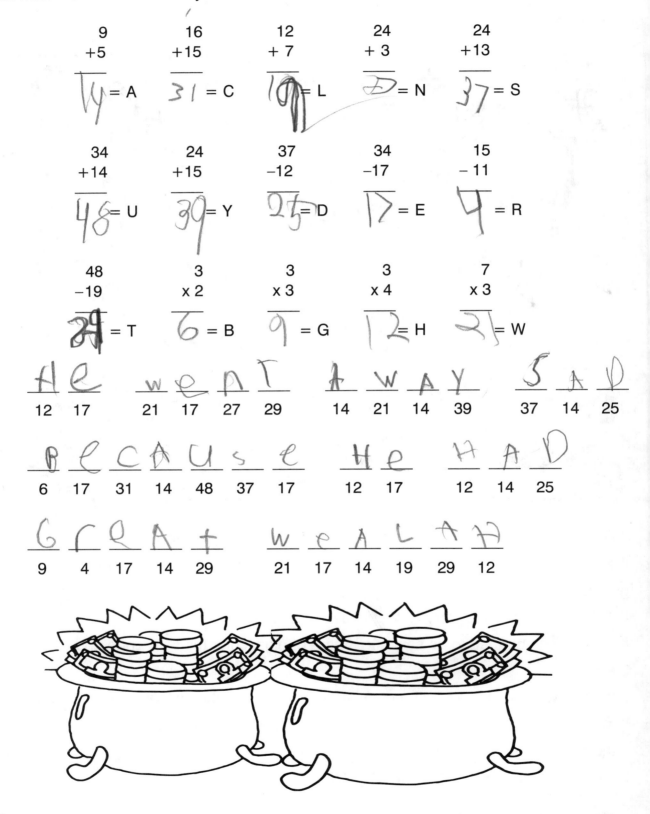

9 +5	16 +15	12 +7	24 +3	24 +13
14 = A	31 = C	19 = L	27 = N	37 = S

34 +14	24 +15	37 -12	34 -17	15 -11
48 = U	39 = Y	25 = D	17 = E	4 = R

48 -19	3 x 2	3 x 3	3 x 4	7 x 3
29 = T	6 = B	9 = G	12 = H	21 = W

H E   W E N T   A W A Y   S A D
12 17   21 17 27 29   14 21 14 39   37 14 25

B E C A U S E   H E   H A D
6 17 31 14 48 37 17   12 17   12 14 25

G R E A T   W E A L T H
9 4 17 14 29   21 17 14 19 29 12

Through the Bible Puzzles, © 2001 by Standard Publishing • Permission granted to photocopy for classroom use only.

A Slave

Read Mark 10:35-38, 40-45. Beginning with column number 1, go down each column until you come to a dot. Copy the letter at the left of the dot onto the first blank.

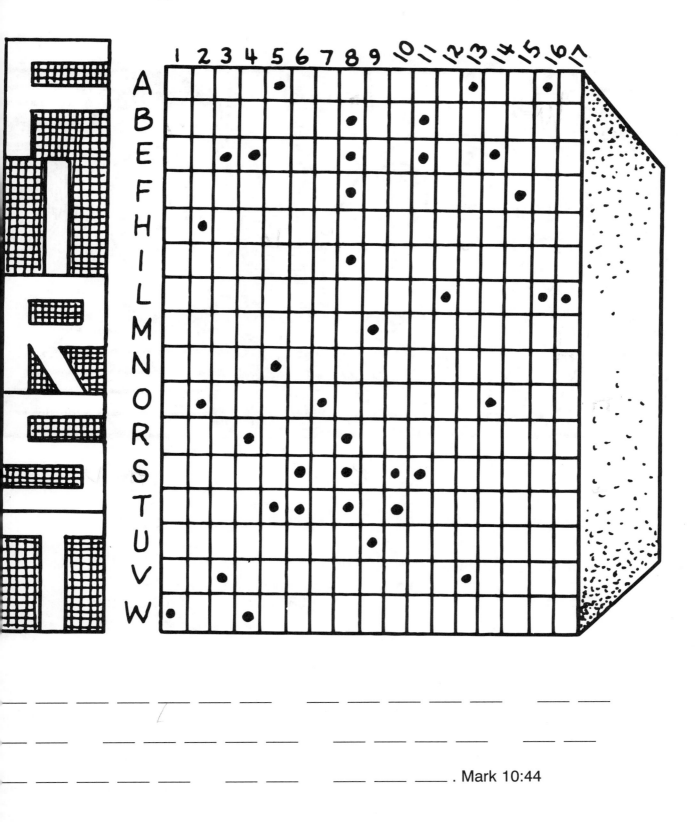

_ _ _ _ _ _ _ _ _ _

_ _ _ _ _ _ _ _

_ _ _ _ _ _ _ _ . Mark 10:44

Through the Bible Puzzles, © 2001 by Standard Publishing • Permission granted to photocopy for classroom use only.

Important Phone Call

Use the telephone dial to find out which commandments Jesus considered most important. Each pair of numbers has a dial number and a letter number. For example, 53 is dial number 5 and the third letter on that dial, L. After you have finished, check your answer by reading Mark 12:30, 31.

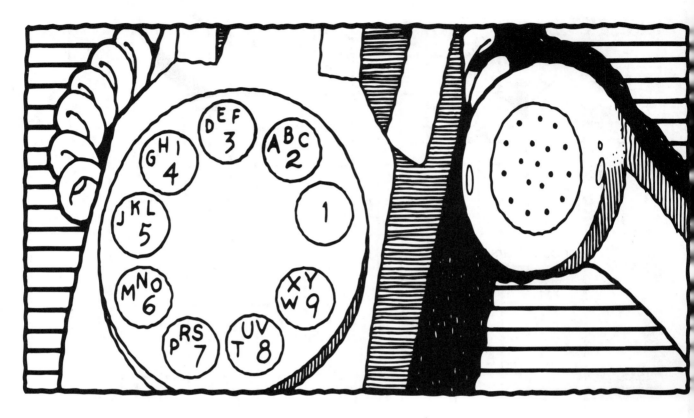

_____ _____ _____ _____
53-63-83-32   81-42-32   53-63-72-31   93-63-82-72

_____ _____ _____ _____
41-63-31   91-43-81-42   21-53-53   93-63-82-72

_____ . _____ _____
42-32-21-72-81   53-63-83-32   93-63-82-72

_____ _____ _____ .
62-32-43-41-42-22-63-72   21-73   93-63-82-72-73-32-53-33

 Through the Bible Puzzles, © 2001 by Standard Publishing • Permission granted to photocopy for classroom use only.

The Widow's Offering

Find out what the widow put in the offering by placing the correct letter in the blank. Check your answer by reading Mark 12:41-44.

1. _____ You'll find me once in *snake* and twice in *elephant*.

2. _____ You'll find me in *vanilla*, but not in *chocolate* or *lemon lime*.

3. _____ I'm once in *ears* and twice in *eyes*.

4. _____ I'm a consonant in *treasure* but not in *stadium*.

5. _____ You'll see me in *yard*, but not in *lard*.

6. _____ Look for me twice in *tight* and *little*.

7. _____ I'm a consonant in *house* and also in *heart*.

8. _____ I'm a vowel in *Illinois* but not in *Oregon*.

9. _____ I'm a consonant found once in *bean* and twice in *banana*.

10. _____ I'm a consonant in *green*, but not in *brown*.

The widow put in ___ ___ ___ ___ ___ ___ ___ ___ ___ ___ .

Through the Bible Puzzles, © 2001 by Standard Publishing • Permission granted to photocopy for classroom use only.

Missing Word ABCs

Turn to Mark 15:21-28, 33-39 to locate the missing words in this list of ABCs.

A __ __ __ __ __ __ __ __   Simon was his father (v. 21).

B __ __ __ __ __   It ripped from top to _____ (v. 38).

C __ __ __ __ __ __   This ripped (v. 38).

D __ __ __ __ __ __ __   What came at the sixth hour (v. 33)?i

E __ __ __ __ __   They thought he called _____ (v. 35).

F __ __ __ __ __ __ __   Jesus thought God had _____ him (v 34).

G __ __ __ __ __ __ __   Where was Jesus taken (v. 22)?

H __ __ __ __   The centurion _____ his cry (v. 39).

I __   Simon was on his way _____ from the country (v. 21).

J __ __ __   Group of people mentioned (v. 26).

K __ __ __   The inscription said he was a _____ (v. 26).

L __ __ __   They cast _____ (v. 24).

M __ __ __ __   The wine was mixed with _____ (v. 23).

N __ __ __ __   The hour mentioned (v. 34).

O __ __ __ __ __ __   Then they _____ him wine (v. 23).

P __ __ __ __ __ __   Simon was just _____ by (v. 21).

R __ __ __ __ __ __   The others crucified were _____ (v. 27).

S __ __ __ __ __   What they filled (v. 36).

T __ __ __ __   The hour mentioned (v. 25).

U __ __ __ __   Darkness covered the land _____ the ninth hour (v. 33).

  Through the Bible Puzzles, © 2001 by Standard Publishing • Permission granted to photocopy for classroom use only.

Alleluia!

Write the words missing from this part of Mark's Gospel in the puzzle boxes. The chapter and verse where the answers are found are at the end of each sentence.

Joseph of (**1**) _____ went boldly to (**2**) _____ and asked for Jesus'

(**3**) _____ (**15:43**).

Joseph (**4**) _____ the body in linen and placed it (**5**) _____ a tomb and rolled a

(**6**) _____ against the (**7**) _____ (**15:46**).

Three women brought (**8**) _____ to anoint (**9**) _____ body (**16:1**).

They saw a young (**10**) _____ dressed in a white (**11**) _____ sitting on the

(**12**) _____ side and they were (**13**) _____ (**16:5**).

Now read the circled letters in your answers to find out what the young man said to the women.

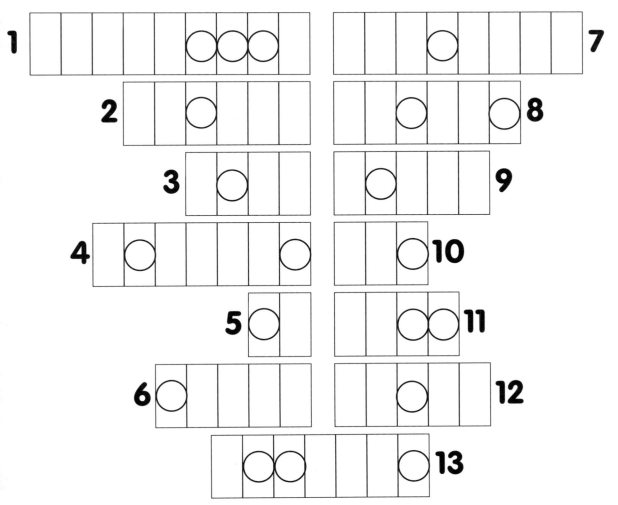

Chrono-Code

Read Luke 1:8-25. Number the sentences below in the order they happened. Then write the letters next to each number on the blanks at the bottom of the page. You will find out what the angel said to Zechariah.

_____ **U**   The worshipers at the temple prayed outside.

_____ **A**   Elizabeth said, "The Lord has done this for me."

_____ **B**   Zechariah returned home.

_____ **O**   The angel said John was not to drink any wine.

_____ **H**   Gabriel said Zechariah would not be able to speak.

_____ **R**   Zechariah was afraid.

_____ **Y**   Zechariah was chosen to burn incense.

_____ **P**   The angel promised the birth of John.

_____ **D**   Zechariah made signs to the people but couldn't speak.

_____ **E**   The people wondered why Zechariah was taking so long.

_____ **N**   Zechariah asked, "How can I be sure of this?"

_____ **S**   An angel appeared in the temple.

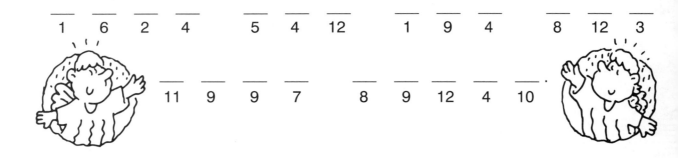

```
___ ___ ___ ___   ___ ___ ___   ___ ___ ___   ___ ___ ___
 1   6   2   4     5   4   12    1   9   4     8   12   3

        ___ ___ ___ ___   ___ ___ ___ ___ ___ .
         11   9   9   7     8   9   12   4   10
```

 Through the Bible Puzzles, © 2001 by Standard Publishing • Permission granted to photocopy for classroom use only.

Read Luke 1:26-28, 30-33, 38-42, 46, 47. Use the code to fill in the missing words.

A	B	C	D	E	G	H	I	J	L

M	N	O	P	R	S	T	U	V	W

THE ANGEL, GABRIEL, SAID TO MARY,

"YOU WILL BE WITH ☐☐☐☐☐

AND GIVE ☐☐☐☐☐ TO A ☐☐☐

☐☐☐☐☐ ." MARY ANSWERED,

I AM THE ☐☐☐☐ ☐ ☐☐☐☐☐☐☐

" MAY IT BE .... AS YOU

HAVE ☐☐☐☐ ."

LUKE 1: 31,38

Through the Bible Puzzles, © 2001 by Standard Publishing • Permission granted to photocopy for classroom use only.

It's a Boy!

Use the code to find out what Zechariah wrote on his tablet. Read Luke 1:57-67 if you need help

___ ___ ___ ___ ___   ___ ___ ___ ___ ___ ___ ___ ___ ___

Through the Bible Puzzles, © 2001 by Standard Publishing • Permission granted to photocopy for classroom use only.

A Savior

Read Luke 2:1-20. Find the angel's message by going through the maze. Then write the letters on the lines below, using only the letters on the correct path to Jesus.

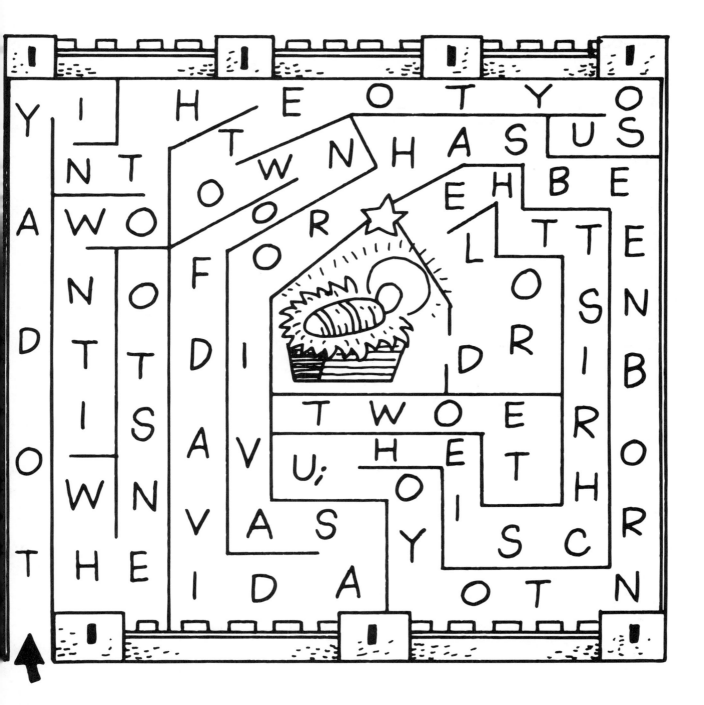

_____

_____

_____

Scrambled Rulers

Unscramble the names and titles of rulers below. Read Luke 2:1-20 if you need help. Then w
the letters over numbers in the blanks with matching numbers at the bottom of the page to fi
important message.

NIRISIQUU ___ ___ ___ ___ ___ ___ ___ ___ ___
                      11   20   6

RACASE ___ ___ ___ ___ ___ ___
        4   15   7

VADID ___ ___ ___ ___ ___
     13 8   3

GUTSUSUA ___ ___ ___ ___ ___ ___ ___ ___
     5   1   14

VOGORNER ___ ___ ___ ___ ___ ___ ___ ___
      2   16   17 18

STRICH ___ ___ ___ ___ ___ ___
     12   9

DORL ___ ___ ___ ___
    10 19

___ ___ ___ ___ _Y_   ___   ___ ___ ___ ___ ___ ___
1   2   3   4   5   6   7   8   9 10 11

___ ___ ___ _B_ ___ ___ ___   _B_ ___ ___ ___!
12 13 14   15 16 17   18 19 20

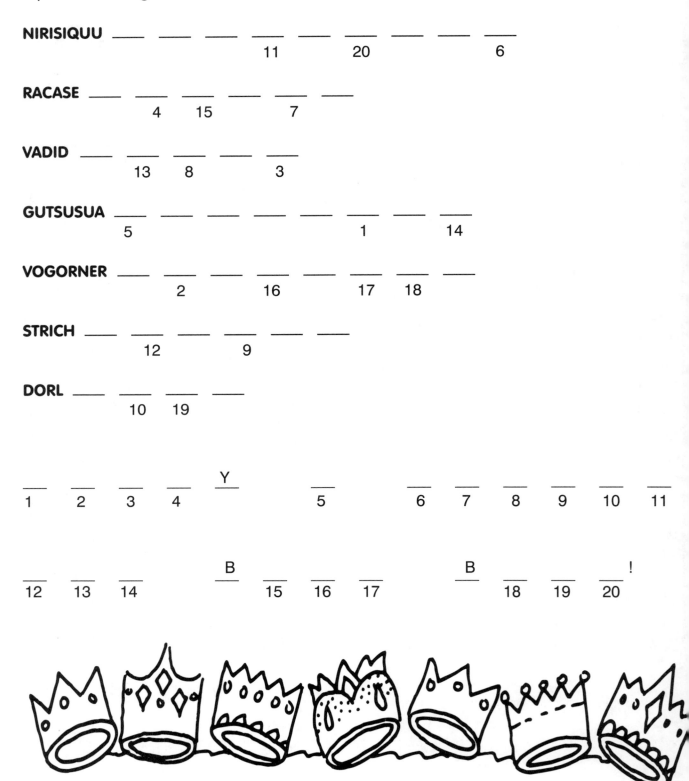

 Through the Bible Puzzles, © 2001 by Standard Publishing • Permission granted to photocopy for classroom use only.

umble John

Unscramble these persons or groups in Luke 3:2, 3, 10-18. Write the letters in the matching shapes at the bottom of the page to find what John preached.

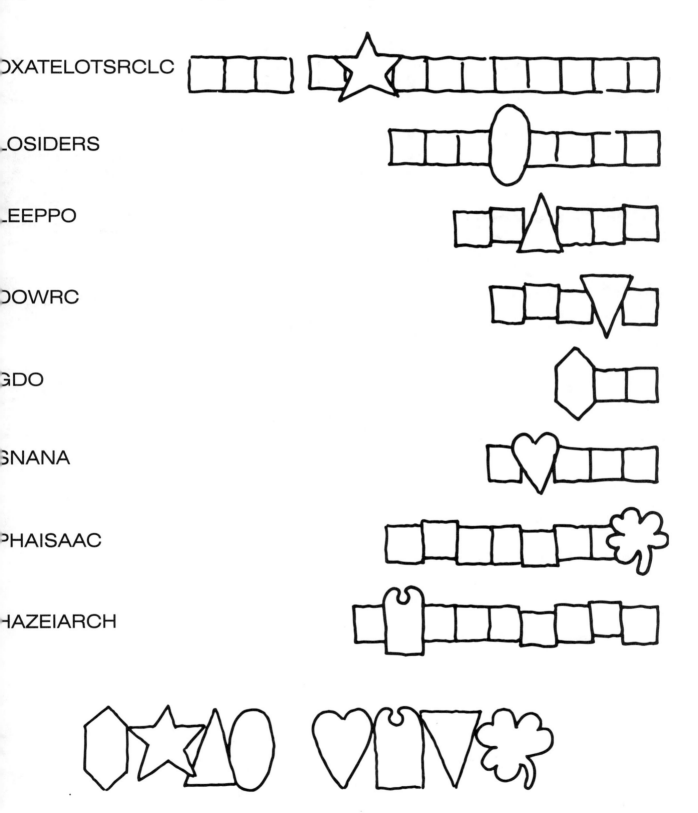

OXATELOTSRCLC

OSIDERS

EEPPO

OOWRC

GDO

SNANA

PHAISAAC

HAZEIARCH

Fishers of Men

Read the Bible story from Luke 5:1-11 which tells the exciting story of Jesus calling his first disciples. Then fill in the puzzle using the clues given.

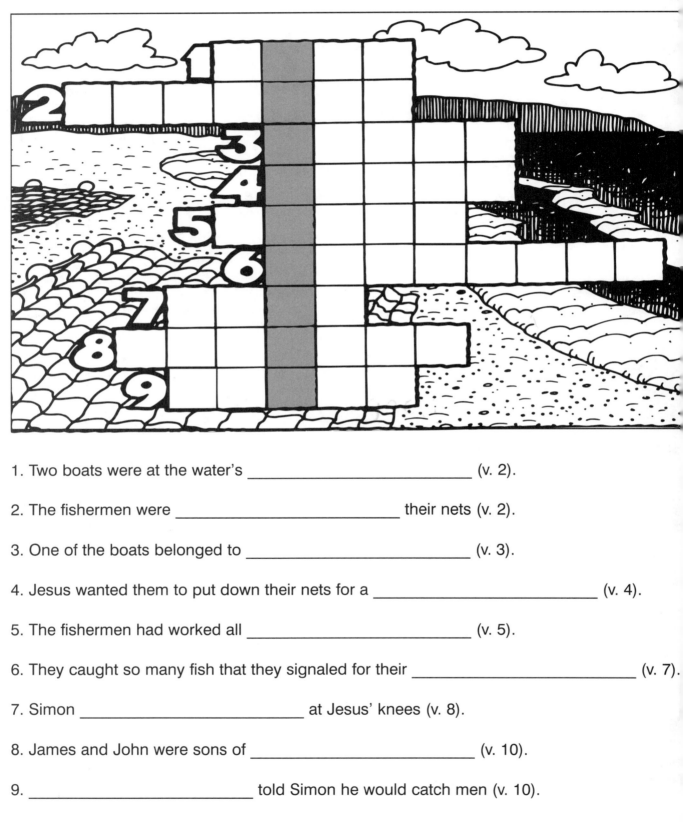

1. Two boats were at the water's _____ (v. 2).

2. The fishermen were _____ their nets (v. 2).

3. One of the boats belonged to _____ (v. 3).

4. Jesus wanted them to put down their nets for a _____ (v. 4).

5. The fishermen had worked all _____ (v. 5).

6. They caught so many fish that they signaled for their _____ (v. 7).

7. Simon _____ at Jesus' knees (v. 8).

8. James and John were sons of _____ (v. 10).

9. _____ told Simon he would catch men (v. 10).

Through the Bible Puzzles, © 2001 by Standard Publishing • Permission granted to photocopy for classroom use only.

The Alabaster Jar

Read Luke 7:36-50. In the puzzle, cross out the twelve words from the story that are listed below. There will be a lot of letters left over but only eight different kinds. Write down each kind once. Then put these eight letters in the correct order to make a word that tells about the woman's sins.

Words: Pharisee, Simon, perfume, feet, tears, hair, sinful, prophet, money, pay, debts, table

The woman's sins were ___ ___ ___ ___ ___ ___ ___ ___ .

Through the Bible Puzzles, © 2001 by Standard Publishing • Permission granted to photocopy for classroom use only.

Good Soil

Read Luke 8:4-8, 11-15. Finish the verse by matching the shapes at the top of the page with the same shapes below.

The seed on good

stands for those with a

and

who hear the

retain it, and by

a .

Luke 8:15

Through the Bible Puzzles, © 2001 by Standard Publishing • Permission granted to photocopy for classroom use only.

Jesus Calms a Stormy Sea

What did the disciples say about Jesus after he calmed a storm? To find out, follow the line from each letter to the empty circle and write the same letter in the circle. Read Luke 8:22-25 for help.

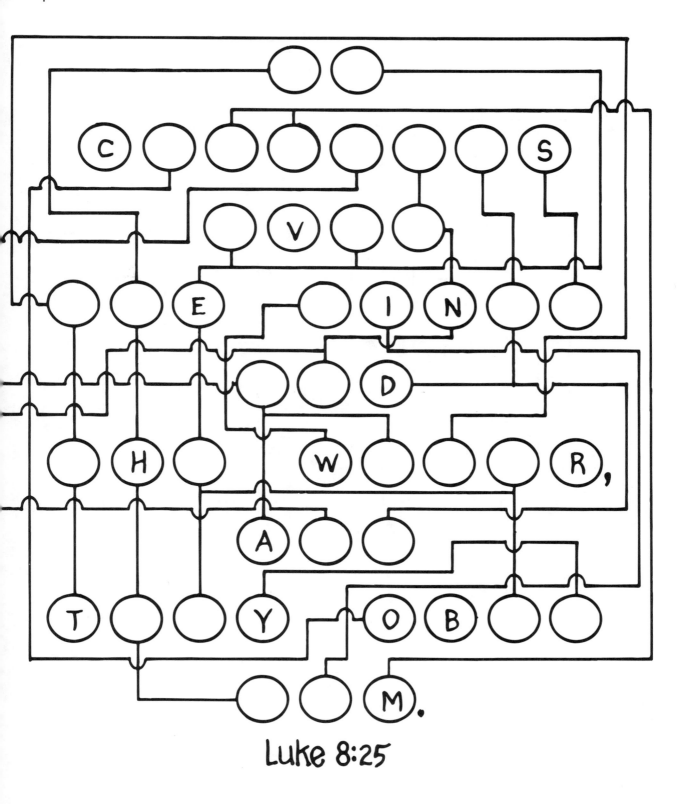

Luke 8:25

Through the Bible Puzzles, © 2001 by Standard Publishing • Permission granted to photocopy for classroom use only.

Just Believe

Read Luke 8:41-55. Starting with column 1, go down each column until you find a dot. Copy the letter to the left of the dot onto the first blank. Fill in the blanks in order.

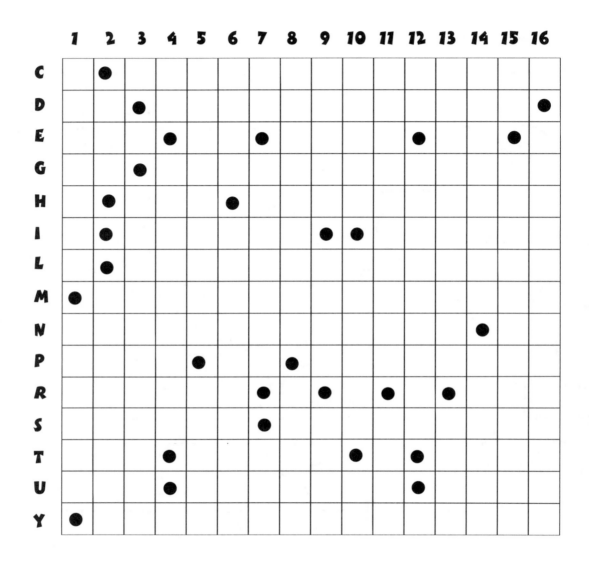

" ____ ____ ____ ____ ____ ____ ____ , ____ ____ ____

____ ____ ! " ____ ____ ____ ____ ____ ____

____ ____ ____ ____ ____ ____ .

Through the Bible Puzzles, © 2001 by Standard Publishing • Permission granted to photocopy for classroom use only.

The Glory of the Lord

Play detective and see if you can spot mistakes in the following statements about the story in Luke 9:28-36. Put a line through the word(s) that are wrong. Above these mistakes, write the correct word(s).

1. About seven days later, Jesus took three men with him into the mountains.

2. The three men were Peter, Andrew, and James.

3. Jesus took these men to the mountains to fast.

4. While Jesus was praying, his hands changed.

5. Jesus' hair became as bright as a flash of lightning.

6. Three people from the time of the Old Testament appeared with Jesus.

7. Peter and the others were not sleepy.

8. While Peter was speaking, a thunderstorm came.

9. They heard a voice speak from the ground.

10. The voice told them Jesus was his Son, and they were to obey him.

11. When they came down from the mountain, they told everyone what they had seen.

A Good Neighbor

Read Luke 10:29-37 and answer the questions. Circle the letter of each correct answer. Find the spaces in section 1 that contain the same letter as the answer to the question #1, and color them in. Do the same with the other three sections.

1. A man was going to Jericho when he fell into whose hands?

a. hermits   **b**. robbers   **c**. soldiers

2. A priest passed by the man. Who else passed by?

a. a merchant   **b**. a Jew   **c**. a Levite

3. Who took pity on the man?

a. a Samaritan   **b**. an innkeeper   **c**. the governor

4. Which of the three was a neighbor to the hurt man?

a. the priest   **b**. the Levite   **c**. the Samaritan

138   Through the Bible Puzzles, © 2001 by Standard Publishing • Permission granted to photocopy for classroom use only.

What Did Martha Open?

Read Luke 10:38-42; Romans 10:17; 15:4. Answer the questions below with the most correct word from the list.

1. At whose feet did Mary sit? _____

2. Martha was worried and _____ .

3. Mary _____ to Jesus.

4. Faith comes from _____ the message.

5. Everything that was written in the past was written to _____ us.

6. Who did the better thing: Martha, Mary, or the disciples? _____

(M)a(r)y   Te(a)(c)h   L(i)st(e)ned

(H)el(p)   Ups(e)(t)   (T)a(l)ked

(H)earin(g)   The (L)or(d)'s   (M)a(r)tha's

Now complete the picture by drawing a line from the first circled letter in answer 1 to the following circled letter and so on through answer 6. The picture you draw is the answer to the title question.

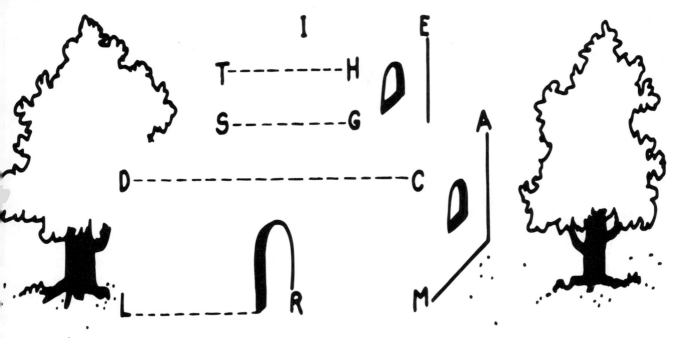

Through the Bible Puzzles, © 2001 by Standard Publishing • Permission granted to photocopy for classroom use only.

Decode the Prayer

Use the code to fill in the missing words and find out what Jesus tells us about prayer. Read Luke 11:1-10 to check your answers.

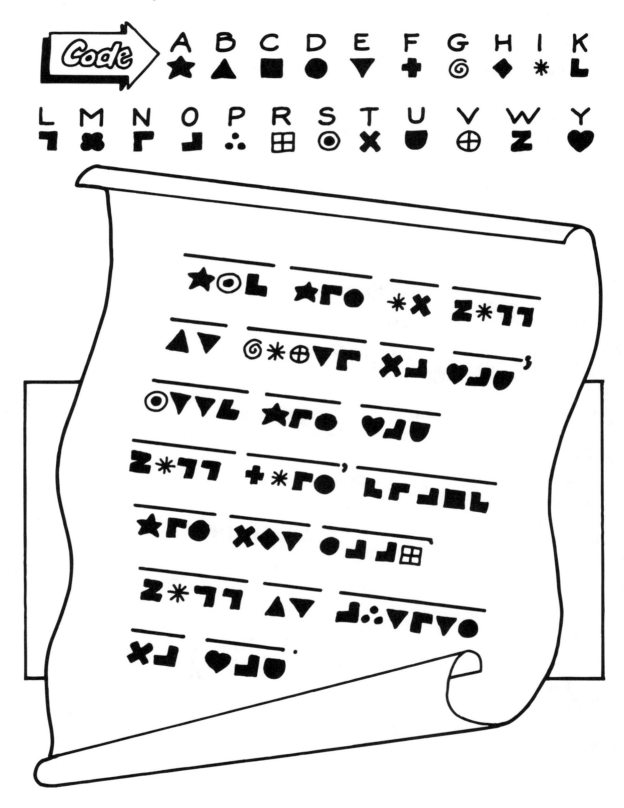

 Through the Bible Puzzles, © 2001 by Standard Publishing • Permission granted to photocopy for classroom use only.

Rich Man

Read Luke 12:16-21. Start with chain #1 and follow the line of letters to find the first word. Write the word in the first blank. Fill in the other words to find out what happened to the rich man.

"But God said to him, 'You _____ ! This very _____ your _____
                            1   2   3

will be _____ from you. Then _____ will _____ what
                    4   5   6

you have _____ for _____?'" "This is how it will be with anyone
                  7   8

who _____ up things for _____ but is not _____ _____
              9   10   11   12

_____ ." Luke 12:20, 21
        13

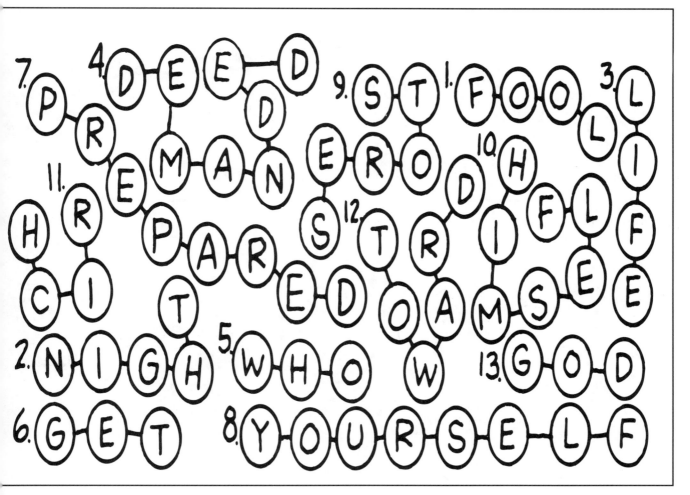

Repent!

Read Luke 15:4-7. Work the rebus to fill in the blanks and complete the verse about repentance.

There will be more rejoicing in heaven over one

__ __ __ __ __ __ __ __ __

who

__ __ __ __ __ __ __ __

than over ninety-nine

__ __ __ __ __ __ __ __ __ __

persons who do not need to repent.

   Through the Bible Puzzles, © 2001 by Standard Publishing • Permission granted to photocopy for classroom use only.

Lost and Found

Identify the pictures below. Starting with picture #1, write the first and last letters of the words you filled in on the blanks below to find what the father did when his lost son came home. Read Luke 15:11-32 to find out more.

_ _ _ drops

shoe _ _ _ _ _

_ _ _ and subtract

And they lived happily ever after. THE _ _ _

sea _ _ _ _ _

_ _ _ _ _ _ _ _ _ _ _ _ _ _

_ _ _ _ _ _ _ _ _ _ _ _ _ .

Through the Bible Puzzles, © 2001 by Standard Publishing • Permission granted to photocopy for classroom use only.

The Rich Man and Lazarus

Read Luke 16:19-31. Use the clues to unscramble the words. Then write the circled letters in order in the spaces at the bottom of the page to find the rich man's request.

(v. 24) the rich man called to _____

MAAHBAR ____ ____ ____ ____ ◯ ____ ____

(v. 20) a beggar named _____

ZARALUS ____ ____ ____ ◯ ____ ____ ____

(v. 28) number of rich man's brothers _____

IFEV ____ ____ ◯ ◯

(v. 19) rich man dressed in _____

ELURPP ◯ ____ ____ ____ ____ ____

(v. 31) _____ to Moses and the Prophets

TINSEL ____ ◯ ____ ◯ ____ ____

(v. 19) rich man lived in _____

RXULUY ____ ____ ____ ____ ____ ◯

(v. 20) Lazarus was covered with _____

ROESS ____ ◯ ____ ____ ____

(v. 31) they will not be _____

CDCNNVIOE ____ ____ ____ ____ ____ ◯ ____ ____ ____

(v. 28) this place of _____

TTREMON ____ ____ ◯ ◯ ____ ____

___ ___ ___ ___ ___   ___ ___ ___ ___   ___ ___ ___   ___ ___ .

   Through the Bible Puzzles, © 2001 by Standard Publishing • Permission granted to photocopy for classroom use only.

Amazingly Healed

Read Luke 17:11-19. Find the answers to the questions by completing the maze.

1. Now on his way to _____ , Jesus traveled along the border between Samaria and Galilee (v. 11).

2. As he was going into a village, _____ _____ who had leprosy met him (v. 12).

3. They called out in a loud voice, "_____, _____ , have pity on us!" (v. 13)

4. When he saw them, he said, "Go, show yourselves to the priests." And as they went, they were _____ (v. 14).

5. One of them, when he saw he was healed, came back, _____ God in a loud voice (v. 15).

6. He threw himself at Jesus' feet and thanked him—and he was a _____ (v. 16).

7. Jesus asked, "Were not all _____ cleansed?" (v. 17).

8. Then he said to him, "Rise and go; your faith has made you _____ " (v. 19).

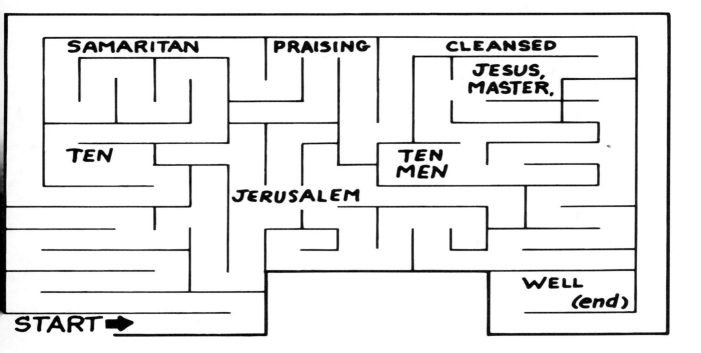

The Pharisee and the Tax Collector

Trace the letters of each maze in order to find what the Pharisee and tax collector said when they prayed to God. Read Luke 18:9-14 to find out more.

   Through the Bible Puzzles, © 2001 by Standard Publishing • Permission granted to photocopy for classroom use only.

A Short Story

Read Luke 19:1-10. Use the clues to unscramble words. Then write the circled letters in order on the spaces at the bottom to learn God's Commandment from Exodus 20:15.

Verse 4. A short man climbed this tree.

MYOSRCEA–fig ___ ◯ ___ ___ ___ ◯ ___ ___

Verse 2. This man wanted to see Jesus.

SCAAZECHU ___ ___ ___ ___ ___ ___ ___ ◯◯

Verse 8. Zacchaeus said if he had done this, he would repay people.

DEECATH ___ ◯ ___ ◯ ___ ___ ___

Verse 2. He was wealthy because of his job as a . . .

ATX ELCORTOLC ___ ___ ___ ___ ___ ◯◯ ___ ___ ___ ___

Verse 5. Jesus told Zacchaeus to . . .

MOEC WODN ___ ___ ___ ___ ___ ___ ◯

Verse 8. He promised to pay back this much.

UROF SMEIT ___ ◯ ___ ___ ◯ ___ ___ ___ ___

Verse 5. Jesus wanted to _____ at Zacchaeus' house.

YTAS ◯◯◯ ___ ___

Verse 1. Jesus entered this city.

CROHIEJ ___ ◯ ___ ___ ___ ___ ___

Verse 9. Zacchaeus received this.

NAITVOASL ___ ◯◯ ___ ___ ___ ___ ___ ___

___ ___.

Through the Bible Puzzles, © 2001 by Standard Publishing • Permission granted to photocopy for classroom use only.

Praise God!

Read Luke 19:28-40 about Jesus' ride into Jerusalem. Then solve the code to find out what the crowd said.

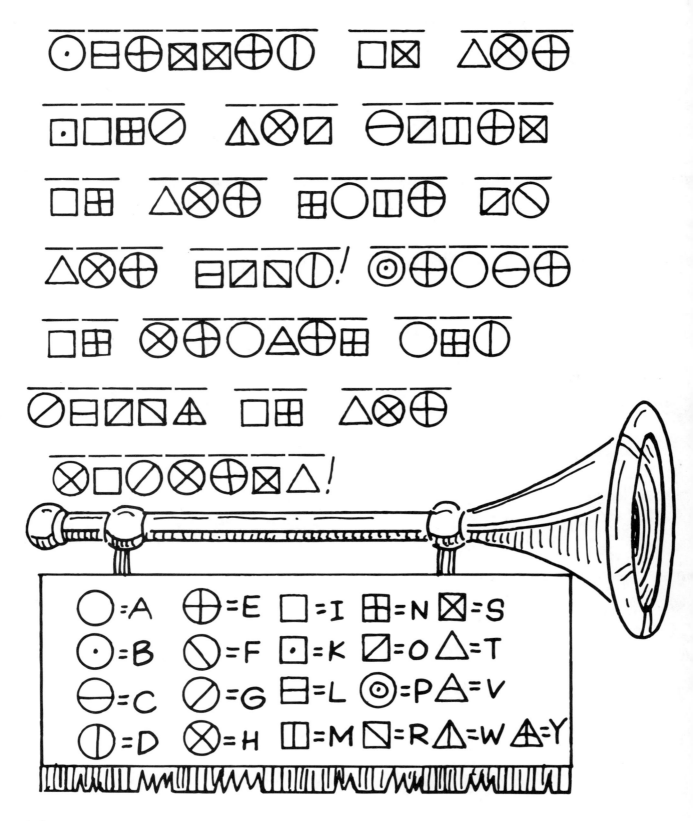

  Through the Bible Puzzles, © 2001 by Standard Publishing • Permission granted to photocopy for classroom use only.

Amazing Love

John 3:16-21 tells about God's amazing love. To solve the puzzle, first work the math problems. Then, beginning with the answer that is 1, write the words in order on the lines below.

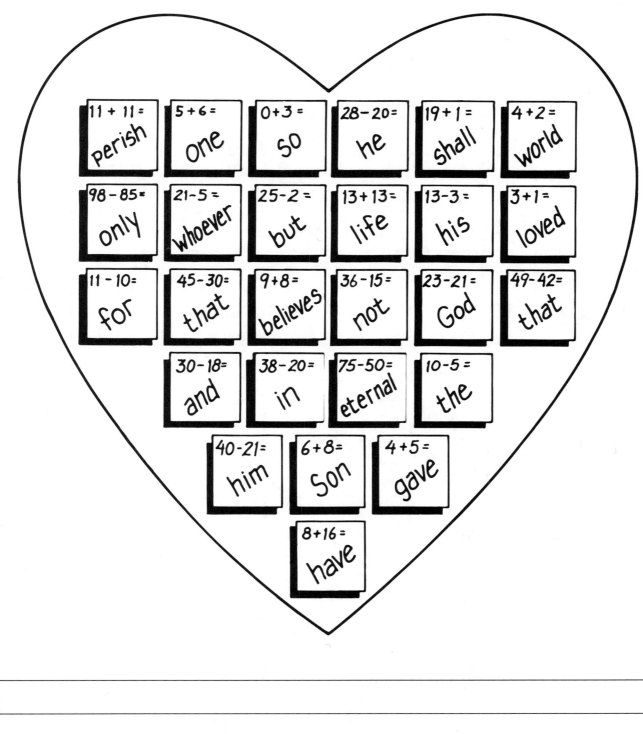

11 + 11 = **perish**	5 + 6 = **one**	0 + 3 = **so**	28 − 20 = **he**	19 + 1 = **shall**	4 + 2 = **world**
98 − 85 = **only**	21 − 5 = **whoever**	25 − 2 = **but**	13 + 13 = **life**	13 − 3 = **his**	3 + 1 = **loved**
11 − 10 = **for**	45 − 30 = **that**	9 + 8 = **believes**	36 − 15 = **not**	23 − 21 = **God**	49 − 42 = **that**
	30 − 18 = **and**	38 − 20 = **in**	75 − 50 = **eternal**	10 − 5 = **the**	
	40 − 21 = **him**	6 + 8 = **Son**	4 + 5 = **gave**		
		8 + 16 = **have**			

_____

_____

_____

_____

Through the Bible Puzzles, © 2001 by Standard Publishing • Permission granted to photocopy for classroom use only.

Worship

Read John 4:19-26. Beginning at one of the lettered boxes, follow the line that leads from it to an empty box and put that letter in the empty box. Fill in the other boxes the same way.

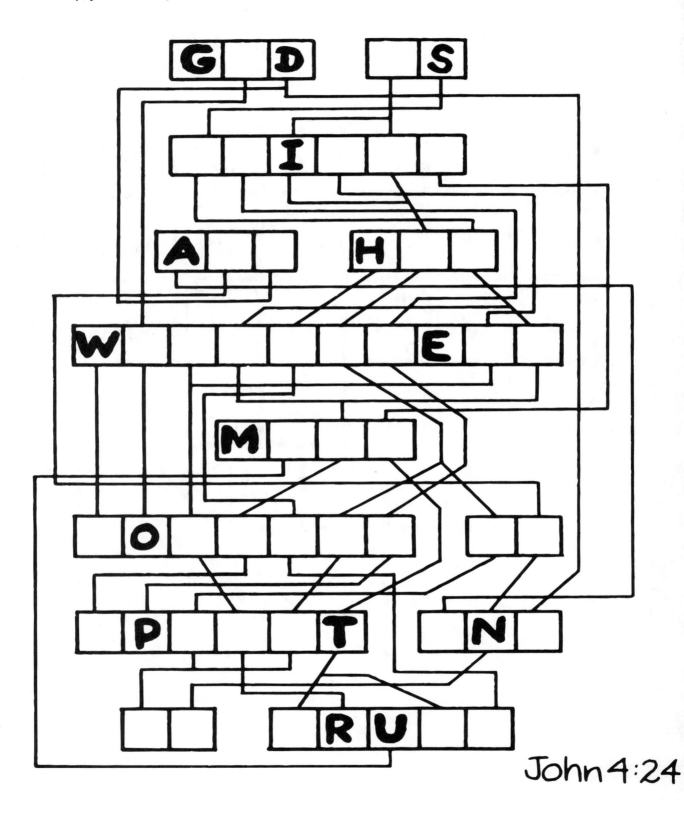

John 4:24

 Through the Bible Puzzles, © 2001 by Standard Publishing • Permission granted to photocopy for classroom use only.

One Lunch That Fed More Than 5,000

What did Andrew ask Jesus about using five loaves and two fishes to feed 5,000 men? How was Andrew's question answered? Use the code to find out. Read John 6:1-13 to find out more.

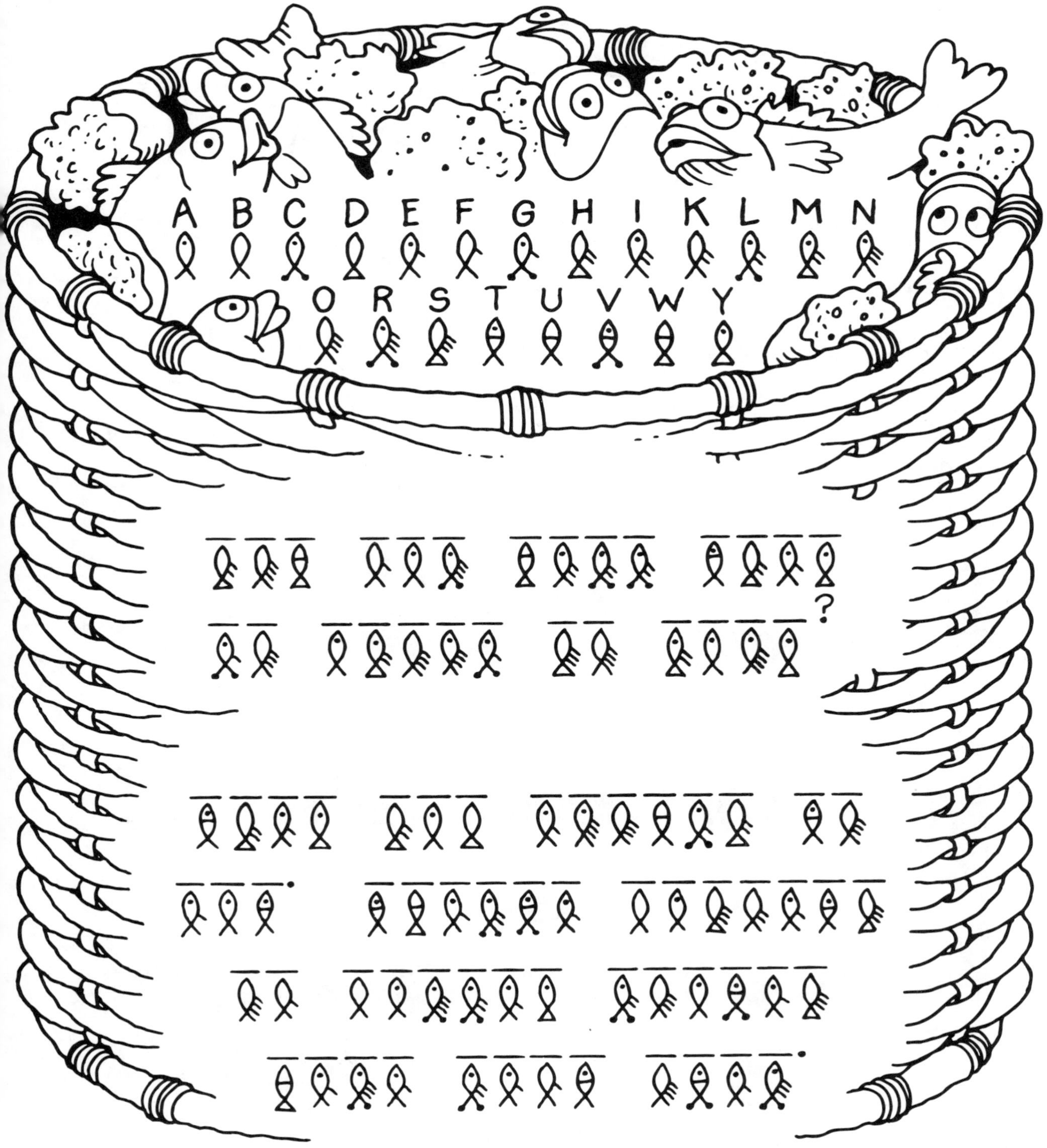

A B C D E F G H I K L M N

O R S T U V W Y

Through the Bible Puzzles, © 2001 by Standard Publishing • Permission granted to photocopy for classroom use only.   151

Lazarus, Come Out!

What happened when Jesus raised Lazarus from the dead? To find the answer, write the words in the matching shapes. Read John 11:32-45.

John 11:45

 Through the Bible Puzzles, © 2001 by Standard Publishing • Permission granted to photocopy for classroom use only.

Jesus Is Risen

1 ————————— ⬥◯⬥ ————————— 🎲

Why did the Jews say Jesus must die (John 19:4-7)?
1. He was from Nazareth.
2. He was a king.
3. He claimed to be the Son of God.

2 ————————— ⬥◯⬥ —————————

The numbers below stand for letters of the alphabet. Which message tells what the notice Pilate wrote about Jesus said (John 19:16-19)?
4. 10, 5, 19, 21, 19, 15, 6   14, 1, 26, 1, 18, 5, 20, 8   11, 9, 14, 7   15, 6   20, 8, 5
   18, 15, 13, 1, 14, 19
5. 10, 5, 19, 21, 19   15, 6   14, 1, 26,1, 18, 5, 20, 8   11, 9, 14, 7   15, 6   20, 8, 5
   10, 5, 23, 19
6. 10, 5, 19, 21, 19   15, 6, 7, 1, 12, 9, 12, 5, 5   11, 9, 14, 7   15, 6   20, 8, 5,
   10, 5, 23, 19

3 ————————— ⬥◯⬥ —————————

Which picture shows how Jesus was given a drink while he was on the cross (John 19:28-30)?

1.    2.    3.

Write the answer number to each puzzle on the spaces below.

1 _____   **2** _____   **3** _____

Change the numbers into these groups of letters and write them on the bottom line.
   1 = hewillc   3 = heisnot   5 = hereheha
   2 = srisen   4 = ntothe   6 = goseewh

Separate these letters into words to find out what the angel said to the women at the tomb (Luke 24:1-7).

_____

Easter Morning

Circle the letter in the true column if the sentence is true. Circle the letter in the false column if the sentence is false. Write the circled letters from top to bottom in the space below for an Easter message. Then read John 20:1-18.

	True	False
1. Mary went to the tomb at sunset.	O	J
2. Mary found the stone rolled away.	E	S
3. The other disciple could run faster than Peter.	S	P
4. The burial clothes were all wrinkled.	N	U
5. Two angels in white were in the tomb.	S	L
6. Peter let the other disciple enter the tomb first.	B	A
7. Mary wept outside the tomb.	R	M
8. Someone told Mary to quit crying.	C	O
9. Mary thought Jesus was a gardener.	S	Q
10. Jesus wanted Mary to hug him.	D	E

___ ___ ___ ___ ___   ___ ___ ___ ___ ___

Through the Bible Puzzles, © 2001 by Standard Publishing • Permission granted to photocopy for classroom use only.

Miraculous Catch of Fish

Find the answers for this maze in John 21:1-14.

1 across   "_____ going out to fish" (v. 3).

2 down   As soon as Simon Peter heard _____ say (v. 7).

3 across   "We'll go _____ you" (v. 3).

3 down   What Peter jumped into (v. 7).

4 across   He was _____ from the dead (v. 14).

5 down   Simon Peter _____ the net ashore (v. 11).

6 across   "No," they _____ (v. 5).

6 down   _____ Jesus appeared again (v. 1).

7 across   Then the _____ whom Jesus loved (v. 7).

Seek the Truth

Read Acts 1:1-12. Then read each sentence below. If a sentence is true, follow the trail in the puzzle from the T. If it is false, follow the trail from the F. Write the word at the end of each trail on the blanks below to spell a message.

		True	False
1.	After his suffering, Jesus showed himself to the apostles and gave proof that he was alive.	T	F
2.	Jesus appeared to them over a period of twenty days.	T	F
3.	Jesus told the apostles to wait for the gift his Father promised.	T	F
4.	Jesus was taken up before their eyes, and the sun hid him from them.	T	F
5.	Two women dressed in blue suddenly appeared.	T	F
6.	Jesus will come back someday in the same way the apostles saw him go into Heaven.	T	F

__ _____ ___ _____

_____ ___ _____

Through the Bible Puzzles, © 2001 by Standard Publishing • Permission granted to photocopy for classroom use only.

Cross It Out

Read Acts 2:1-4, 14, 36-41. Follow the directions below.

1. Cross out 4 words describing the Holy Spirit.
2. Cross out 1 preacher.
3. Cross out 1 feast.
4. Cross out 1 city.
5. Cross out 3 things Peter asked the crowd to do.
6. Cross out 1 number.
7. Cross out 1 nation.
8. Cross out 2 words for the disciples.
9. Cross out 3 things the crowd did.
10. Cross out 1 group of people.

WIND	GOD	REPENT	ELEVEN	MADE
BE BAPTIZED	JESUS	FIRE	SAVE YOURSELVES	PETER
APOSTLES	PENTECOST	SOUND	BOTH	ISRAEL
LORD	TONGUES	JERUSALEM	HEARD	JEWS
ACCEPTED	AND	3000	CHRIST	WERE BAPTIZED

Read the leftover words from left to right and top to bottom to learn Peter's message.

Through the Bible Puzzles, © 2001 by Standard Publishing • Permission granted to photocopy for classroom use only.

Finding Words

The answers to the clues below all end with ING. Use the word clues in the puzzle to fill in the squares with words from Acts 2:42-47.

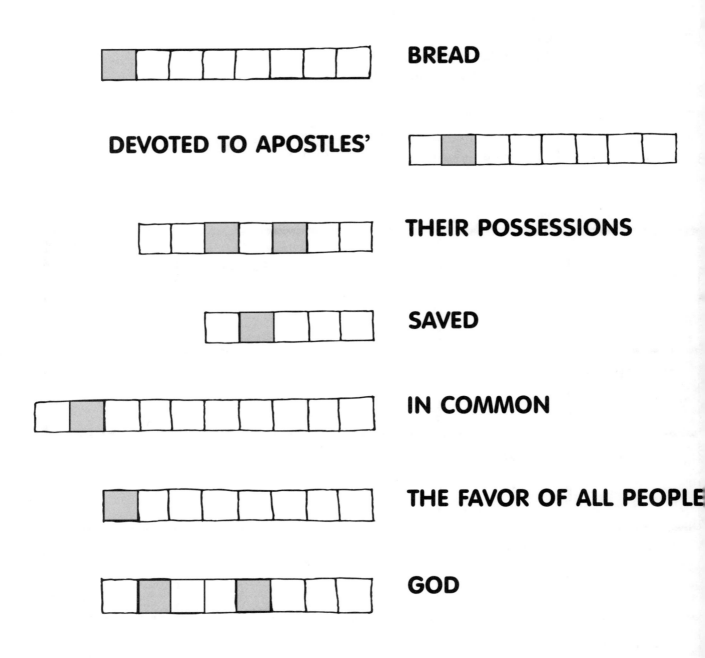

BREAD

DEVOTED TO APOSTLES'

THEIR POSSESSIONS

SAVED

IN COMMON

THE FAVOR OF ALL PEOPLE

GOD

Write the letters from the shaded squares in order to learn who the phrases describe.

_____

    Through the Bible Puzzles, © 2001 by Standard Publishing • Permission granted to photocopy for classroom use only.

What Did the People Think?

Find out by filling in the missing words from Acts 3:1-10. Then write the letters in the blanks below with the same numbers.

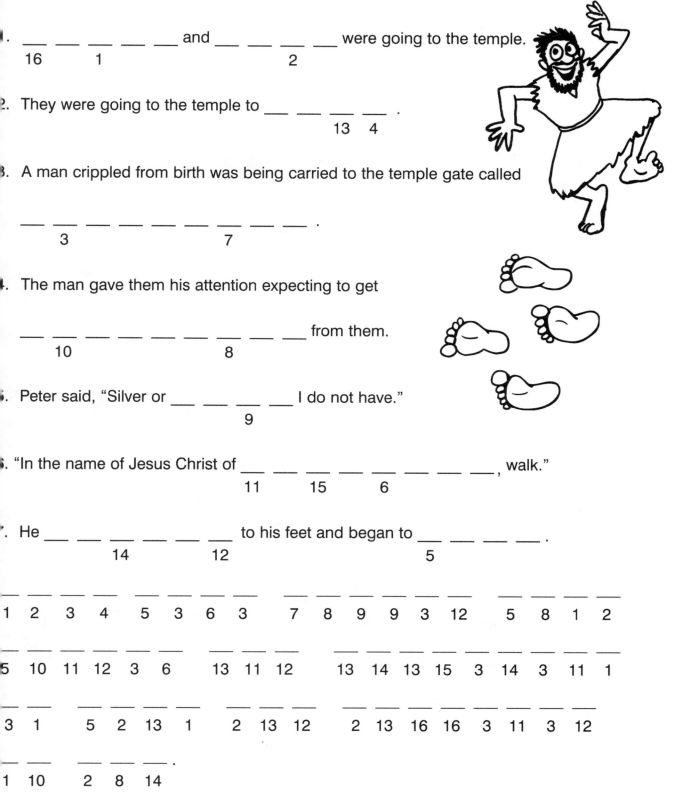

1. __ __ __ __ __ and __ __ __ __ were going to the temple.
   16   1   2

2. They were going to the temple to __ __ __ __ .
                                      13   4

3. A man crippled from birth was being carried to the temple gate called
   __ __ __ __ __ __ __ __ __ __ __ .
      3   7

4. The man gave them his attention expecting to get
   __ __ __ __ __ __ __ __ __ from them.
      10   8

5. Peter said, "Silver or __ __ __ __ I do not have."
                          9

6. "In the name of Jesus Christ of __ __ __ __ __ __ __ __ , walk."
                                    11   15   6

7. He __ __ __ __ __ __ to his feet and began to __ __ __ __ .
         14   12   5

__ __ __ __ __ __ __ __   __ __ __ __ __ __   __ __ __ __
1 2 3 4 5 3 6 3   7 8 9 9 3 12   5 8 1 2

__ __ __ __ __ __   __ __ __   __ __ __ __ __ __ __ __ __
5 10 11 12 3 6   13 11 12   13 14 13 15 3 14 3 11 1

__ __   __ __ __ __   __ __ __   __ __ __ __ __ __ __ __
3 1   5 2 13 1   2 13 12   2 13 16 16 3 11 3 12

__ __   __ __ __ .
1 10   2 8 14

On Trial

During a trial, the jury looks at all the evidence and doesn't use information that doesn't affect the problem. Cross out from this list of evidence the following words:

1. Names of Old Testament books of the Bible.
2. Names of cities found in the Bible.
3. Names of animals found in the Bible.
4. Names of women found in the Bible.

Genesis	Peter	Esther	and
John	Proverbs	were	arrested
Jerusalem	for	talking	Jericho
sheep	about	Daniel	Jesus.
Mary	Peter	Bethany	said
the	people	had	crucified
Psalms	Jesus.	The	rulers
were	lion	donkey	astonished
Bethlehem	at	the	Martha
courage	Peter	and	John
showed	but	warned	goat
them	not	Jonah	to
Ruth	speak	of	Jesus.

The leftover words reading from left to right tell about a problem Peter and John faced in Acts 4:1-20.

 Through the Bible Puzzles, © 2001 by Standard Publishing • Permission granted to photocopy for classroom use only.

What's in a Name?

The clues for this puzzle come from Acts 4:32-36. Rearrange the circled letters to find what the name of Barnabas means.

1. These were of one heart and mind (v. 32).

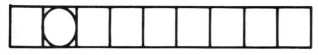

2. What they did with their things (v. 32).

3. The kind of power they had (v. 33).

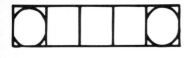

4. The apostles continued to do this (v. 33).

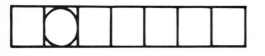

5. What special thing they told about Jesus (v. 33).

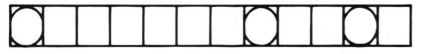

6. They didn't have any person like this (v. 34).

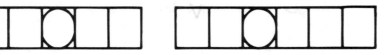

7. The two things people sold (v. 34).

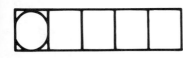

8. What people brought to apostles from selling lands and houses (vv. 34, 35).

SON OF

Stephen's Last Stand

Read Acts 6:8-11; 7:54-60. Find the listed words in the puzzle. When you find a word, color the letter squares blue if the word relates to Stephen. Color them red if the word relates to the members of the synagogue.

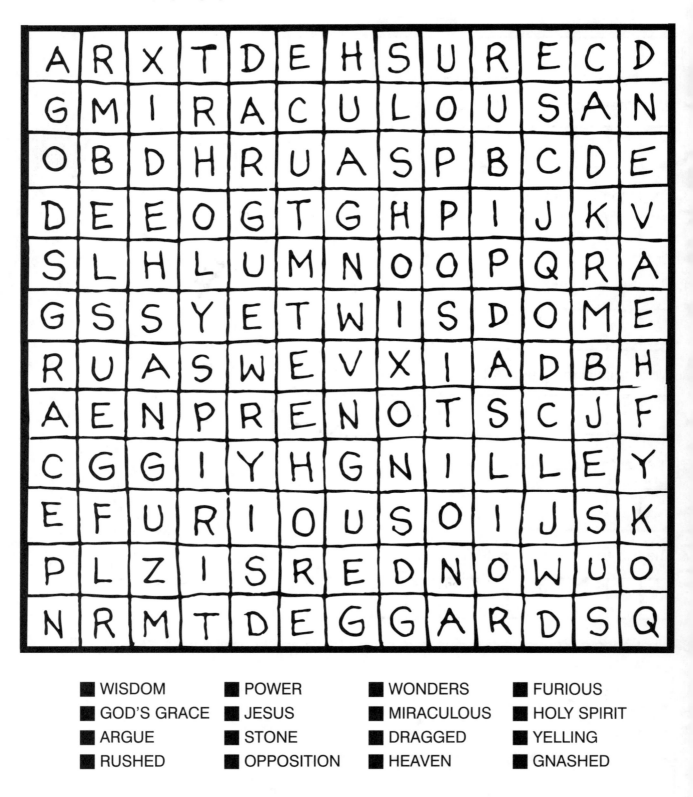

A	R	X	T	D	E	H	S	U	R	E	C	D
G	M	I	R	A	C	U	L	O	U	S	A	N
O	B	D	H	R	U	A	S	P	B	C	D	E
D	E	E	O	G	T	G	H	P	I	J	K	V
S	L	H	L	U	M	N	O	O	P	Q	R	A
G	S	S	Y	E	T	W	I	S	D	O	M	E
R	U	A	S	W	E	V	X	I	A	D	B	H
A	E	N	P	R	E	N	O	T	S	C	J	F
C	G	G	I	Y	H	G	N	I	L	L	E	Y
E	F	U	R	I	O	U	S	O	I	J	S	K
P	L	Z	I	S	R	E	D	N	O	W	U	O
N	R	M	T	D	E	G	G	A	R	D	S	Q

- ■ WISDOM
- ■ GOD'S GRACE
- ■ ARGUE
- ■ RUSHED
- ■ POWER
- ■ JESUS
- ■ STONE
- ■ OPPOSITION
- ■ WONDERS
- ■ MIRACULOUS
- ■ DRAGGED
- ■ HEAVEN
- ■ FURIOUS
- ■ HOLY SPIRIT
- ■ YELLING
- ■ GNASHED

Through the Bible Puzzles, © 2001 by Standard Publishing • Permission granted to photocopy for classroom use only.

The Ethiopian's Question

Cross out every C, F, G, J, Q, V, and X. Write the remaining letters in order on the blanks below to find the question the Ethiopian asked Philip in Acts 8:36.

```
L   C   V   F   Q   O   J   C   X   O
V   K   V   J   C   H   F   J   Q   E
R   V   X   E   X   C   F   I   G   S
V   X   W   J   A   G   J   T   C   Q
E   G   F   R   V   J   Q   W   C   H
J   G   F   Y   Q   J   C   S   V   J
H   X   C   O   C   G   U   F   G   V
L   C   X   D   F   Q   N   J   C   J
T   V   Q   I   J   C   F   B   C   Q
E   X   F   B   G   F   V   A   J   P
G   T   C   I   J   C   Z   V   E   J
C   V   X   D   Q   V   J   C   G   F
```

__ __ __ __ __ , __ __ __ __ __ __ __ __ __ __ __ .

__ __ __ __ __ , __ __ __ __ __ __ __ __

__ __ __ __ __ __ __ __ ?

Saul's Conversion

Remember Paul was called Saul before his conversion. Saul was blinded by a light during his conversion. Use the braille chart to decode the missing words. (See Acts 9:1-19.)

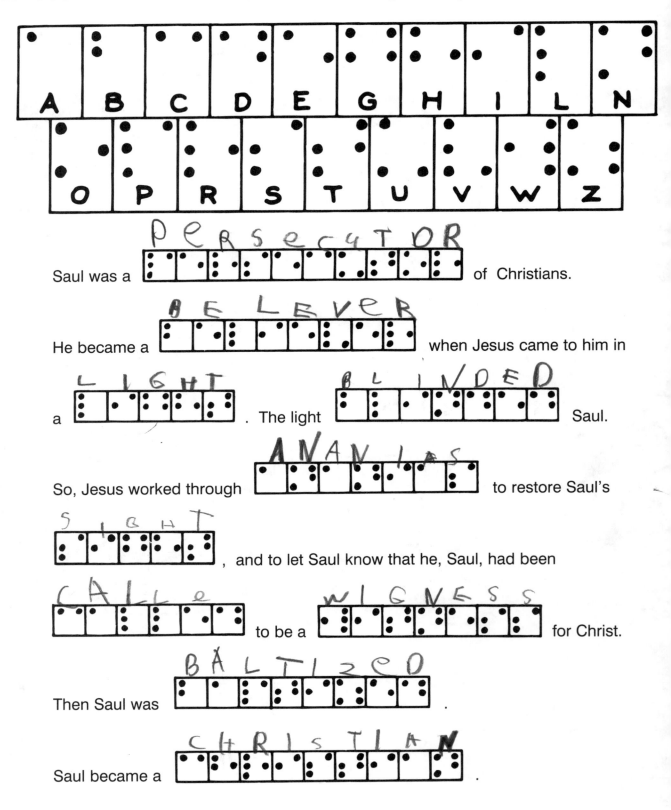

Saul was a **PERSECUTOR** of Christians.

He became a **BELIEVER** when Jesus came to him in

a **LIGHT**. The light **BLINDED** Saul.

So, Jesus worked through **ANANIAS** to restore Saul's

SIGHT, and to let Saul know that he, Saul, had been

CALLE to be a **WITNESS** for Christ.

Then Saul was **BAPTIZED**.

Saul became a **CHRISTIAN**.

Through the Bible Puzzles, © 2001 by Standard Publishing • Permission granted to photocopy for classroom use only.

Joy in Joppa

Read Acts 9:36-42. Use the code and the word clues to fill in the boxes.

■ = b, d, f, h, k, l, t

□ = g, j, p, q, y

▨ = c, m, n, r, s, v, w, x, z

▢ = a, e, i, o, u

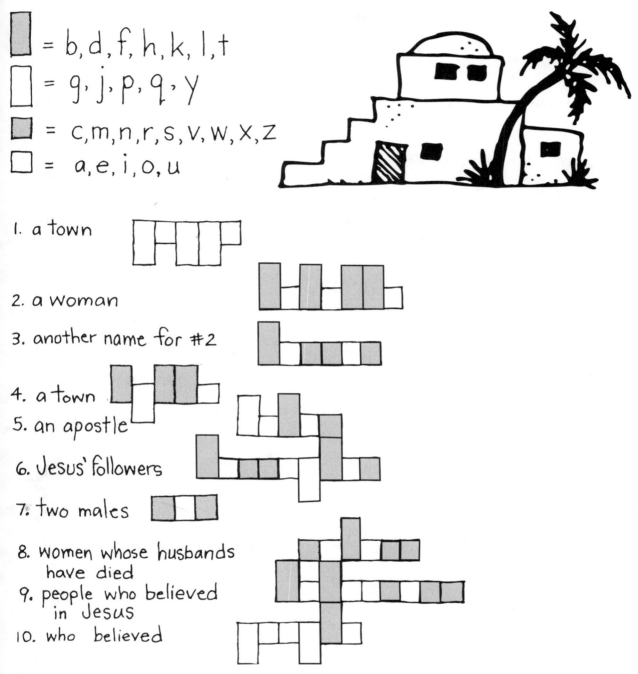

1. a town

2. a woman

3. another name for #2

4. a town

5. an apostle

6. Jesus' followers

7. two males

8. women whose husbands have died

9. people who believed in Jesus

10. who believed

Read Acts 9:42. Use the code to learn the result of God's miracle in Joppa.

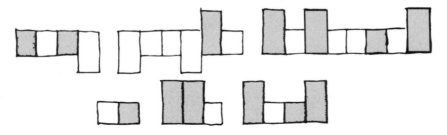

Through the Bible Puzzles, © 2001 by Standard Publishing • Permission granted to photocopy for classroom use only.

Right or Wrong?

Read Acts 10:9-20, 24-28. Read the sentences. If the sentence is true, circle the word in the right column. If the sentence is false, circle the word in the wrong column. Then write the circled words in order at the bottom of the page to learn what God taught Peter.

		Right	**Wrong**
1.	Peter went down in the basement to pray.	Simon	Peter
2.	Peter fell into a trance and saw Heaven open.	learned	taught
3.	Peter saw a large sheet full of four-footed animals, reptiles, and birds.	not	people
4.	A voice told Peter to get up and look at the animals.	about	to
5.	After the vision, four men came looking for Peter.	names	call
6.	The men came from Simon the soldier.	and	any
7.	Peter went with the men to Caesarea to meet Cornelius.	man	sang
8.	Cornelius saw Peter and bowed before him.	sad	impure
9.	Peter talked with Cornelius and a large group of people in his house.	or	songs
10.	It was against the Jewish law for Peter to visit a Gentile.	unclean	always

 Through the Bible Puzzles, © 2001 by Standard Publishing • Permission granted to photocopy for classroom use only.

Christians Scatter

Put the first letter of the name of each picture below the picture. Work the map as the directions are given to you. Read Acts 11:19-30.

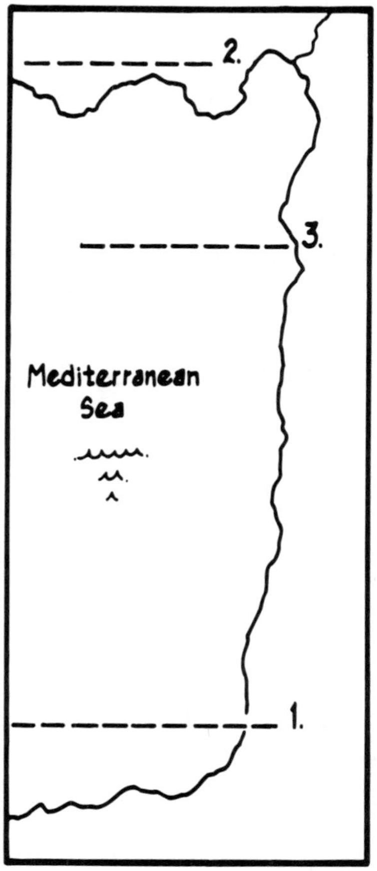

The Christians scattered from Jerusalem because of the stoning of

_ _ _ _ _ _ _ _ .

(Put Jerusalem on the map at point 1.)

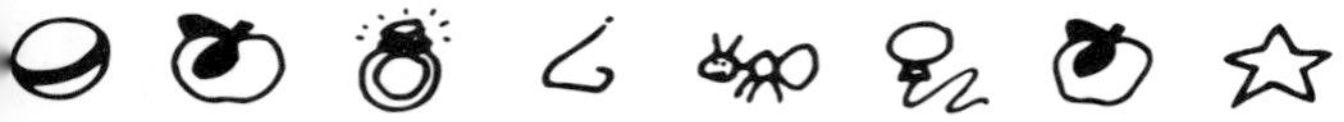

_ _ _ _ _ _ _ _

went to Tarsus to look for Saul. (Put Tarsus at point 2.)
Barnabas and Saul worked one year at

_ _ _ _ _ _ _ .

The disciples were first called

_ _ _ _ _ _ _ _ _ _ _

at Antioch. (Put Antioch at point 3.)
Because of a famine the

_ _ _ _ _ _ _ _ _ _

at Antioch provided help for the brothers in Judea.

Mediterranean
Sea

Good News!

Read Acts 13:1-3, 14-16, 26-33. Use the food code to fill in the blanks.

1. The church at Antioch set apart Barnabas and Corn-apple-cantaloupe-cauliflower.

   _____

2. The church worshiped and nectarine-apple-corn-watermelon-grapefruit-kiwi.

   _____

3. At Pisidian Antioch, Paul and Barnabas were asked to corn-spinach-

   grapefruit-apple-pea. _____

4. Paul told the men in the synagogue about Bean-grapefruit-corn-cantaloupe-corn.

   _____

5. Paul told them that God raised Jesus from kiwi-grapefruit-apple-watermelon-cherry.

   _____

Now use the code to tell a friend what Paul and Barnabas told the people.

_____   _____   _____   _____
Peach — cabbage — cabbage — kiwi

_____   _____   _____   _____
Lettuce — grapefruit — zucchini — corn

CODE:

A	apple
D	kiwi
E	grapefruit
F	nectarine
G	peach
H	cherry
J	bean
K	pea
L	cauliflower
N	lettuce
O	cabbage
P	spinach
S	corn
T	watermelon
U	cantaloupe
W	zucchini

 Through the Bible Puzzles, © 2001 by Standard Publishing • Permission granted to photocopy for classroom use only.

Paul and Barnabas

Read Acts 14:8-20. Go through the maze and put the letters from the path on the line provided. Then use the code to find out what Paul and Barnabas told the people.

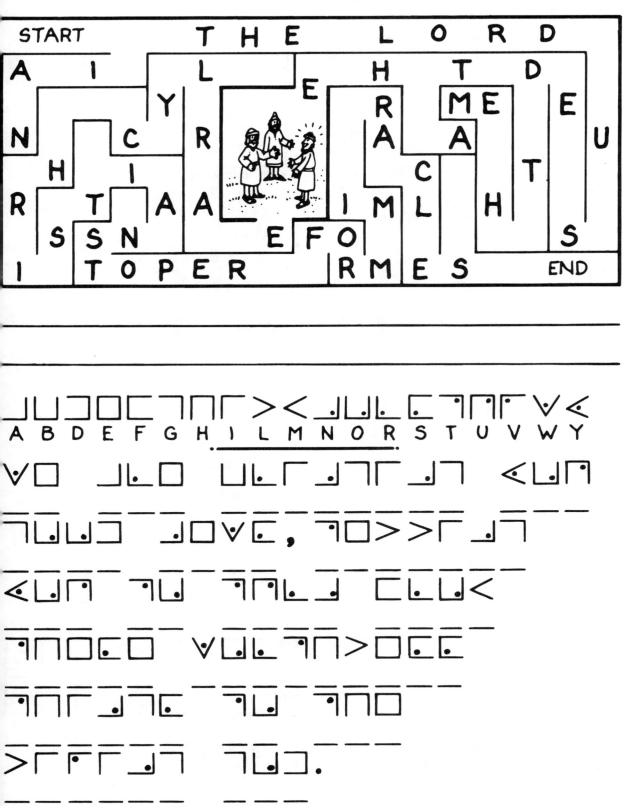

START

| | T | H | E | | L | O | R | D |
|A|I| | | | | | | |
|N| |Y| |E| |H| |T| D|
		C		R		R		ME		E
H			I		R	A		A		U
R	T	A	A				C		H	T
S	S	N			I	M	L		
I			E	F	O				S
	T	O	P	E	R		R	M	E	S	END

_____

_____

A B D E F G H I L M N O R S T U V W Y

Through the Bible Puzzles, © 2001 by Standard Publishing • Permission granted to photocopy for classroom use only.

169

Prison

Read Acts 16:25-34 about Paul and Silas in prison. To find the good that came out of their being in jail, take the letters from the jail house and put them in the empty space below the boxes with the same numbers.

9	10	14	■	2	3	1	11	14	8	■	3	6	15	■	10	1	5
			■							■				■			

4	3	16	1	11	12	■	7	14	8	14	■	5	3	17	14	15
						■					■					

 Through the Bible Puzzles, © 2001 by Standard Publishing • Permission granted to photocopy for classroom use only.

The Unknown God

Read Acts 17:22-31. To find out what Paul told the people in Athens, write the letter of the alphabet that comes before the letter shown in the box above each letter.

Paul told the people about these things:

1. How God raised Jesus

 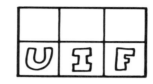 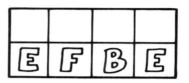

2. How God made the whole

3. How God is Lord of

and

4. How God made every

from one

5. How in God we live and move and

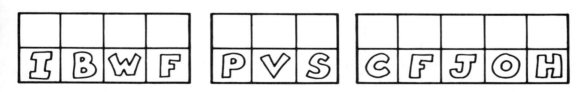

Spreading the Word

Read Acts 19:13-20. Decode the first two sentences by matching the symbols in the sentences to the symbols on the chart. Write the letter that matches the symbol.

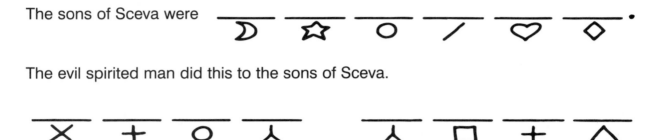

The sons of Sceva were ___ ___ ___ ___ ___ ___ ___ .

The evil spirited man did this to the sons of Sceva.

___ ___ ___ ___   ___ ___ ___ ___

To find the rest of the message, begin with column #1. Go down the column until you come to a shaded box. Copy the letter that is found to the left of the shaded box on the first blank. Do this for each column. Some columns will have more than one letter.

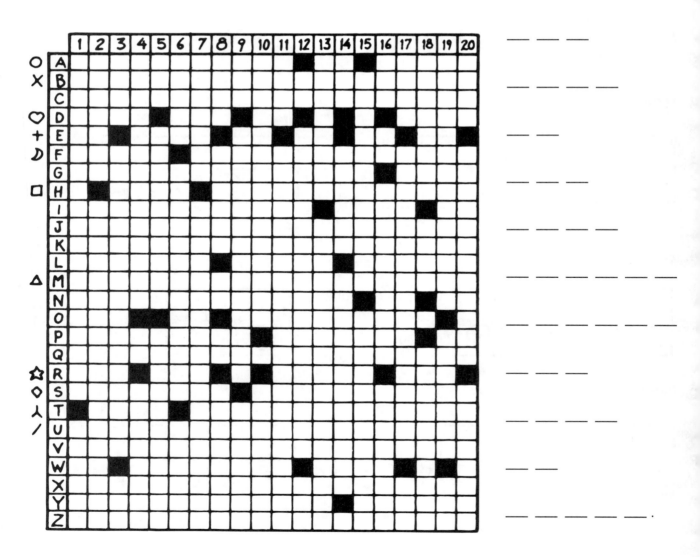

Through the Bible Puzzles, © 2001 by Standard Publishing • Permission granted to photocopy for classroom use only.

Paul's Mission

Read Acts 20:17-32. Use the word clues to unscramble the answers. Then write the circled letters in order in the spaces at the bottom of the page to learn Paul's mission.

Verse 17. Paul traveled from this city.

LEIUMTS __ __ __ __ ◯ __ __

Verse 17. Paul talked to these men.

EEDLRS ◯ ◯ __ __ __ __

Verse 19. Paul served the Lord with this.

ILMIHUY __ __ __ __ ◯ __ ◯ __

Verse 23. Paul was warned by him.

LOYH RIITSP ◯ __ __ __ __ __ __ __ __ __

Verse 21. Paul preached to these people.

EWJ, KREEGS __ ◯ __ __ , ◯ __ __ __ __

Verse 23. Paul faced this problem.

NOSIRP __ __ __ __ ◯ __

Verse 21. Paul wanted everyone to turn to him.

OGD __ ◯ ◯

Verse 24. Paul considered his life this.

GITHONN __ __ __ __ __ ◯ __

Verse 28. Paul told the elders to be these.

REDHEPSSH __ __ ◯ __ __ __ __ __ __

Verse 28. Paul told the elders to keep this.

CHATW ◯ __ __ __ __

Verse 31. Paul warned them with these.

REATS __ __ __ __ ◯

__ __ __ __ __ __ __ __ __ __ __ __ __ __ __ __ __ __

Shipwreck

To find out what Paul told the others on the boat before the shipwreck, color in the empty spaces. Read Acts 27:13-25, 41-44.

Through the Bible Puzzles, © 2001 by Standard Publishing • Permission granted to photocopy for classroom use only.

Love, Love, Love

Read Romans 12:9-19. Match the words or phrases in the flowers to the correct flower pot by drawing a stem. You will learn how God can make your life a "bed of roses."

The Lord's Supper

Read 1 Corinthians 11:23-29, 31, 32. Solve the math problems in each box. Circle the words in the box if the math solution is 15. Write the circled words in order at the bottom of the page to learn why Jesus asked us to observe the Lord's Supper.

8+4+4= JESUS	4+3+8= DO	10-4+2= BREAD	15-1+2= BODY
10-2+7= THIS	1+10+3= DRINK	14-5+4= NIGHT	5+5+5= IN
6+10-1= REMEM- BRANCE	6+8+2= PROCLAIM	4+3+7= EAT	9-2+6= BLOOD
15-5+5= OF	16-2+3= CUP	2+3+4= THANKS	9+9-3= ME

__ __ __ __ _____ ____

__ _____ _____ __ __ ___ __ .

Through the Bible Puzzles, © 2001 by Standard Publishing • Permission granted to photocopy for classroom use only.

Mixed Fruit

The fruit below is mixed up. Write the letters from the apples on the first set of blanks below to find one fruit of the Spirit. Then do the same for the oranges, lemons, bananas, pineapples, strawberries, grapes, raspberries, and pears. The first fruit shown is an apple, the second is an orange, the third is a lemon, and so on, to help you know which fruit is which. Read Galatians 5:22, 23.

___ ___ ___ ___ , ___ ___ ___ ___ , ___ ___ ___ ___ ___ ___ ___ ___ ,

___

___ ___ ___ ___ ___ ___ ___ ___ ___ ___ , ___ ___ ___ ___ ___ ___ ___

___ ___ ___ ___ ___ ___ ___ ___ , ___ ___ ___ ___ ___ ___ ___ ___ ___ ,

___ ___ ___ ___ ___ ___ ___ ___ ___ ___ ___ ___ ___ ___ ,

___ ___ ___ ___ ___ ___ ___ ___ ___ ___ ,

___

___ ___ ___ ___ ___ ___ ___ ___ ___ ___ ___ ___ ___ ___ ___ ___ .

Helpful Crutches

Romans 3:23 tells us that we are spiritually injured because we have sinned. How can we hope to be saved if we cannot walk perfectly, keeping all God's commandments? Use the helpful crutches to solve the message of hope from Ephesians 2:8.

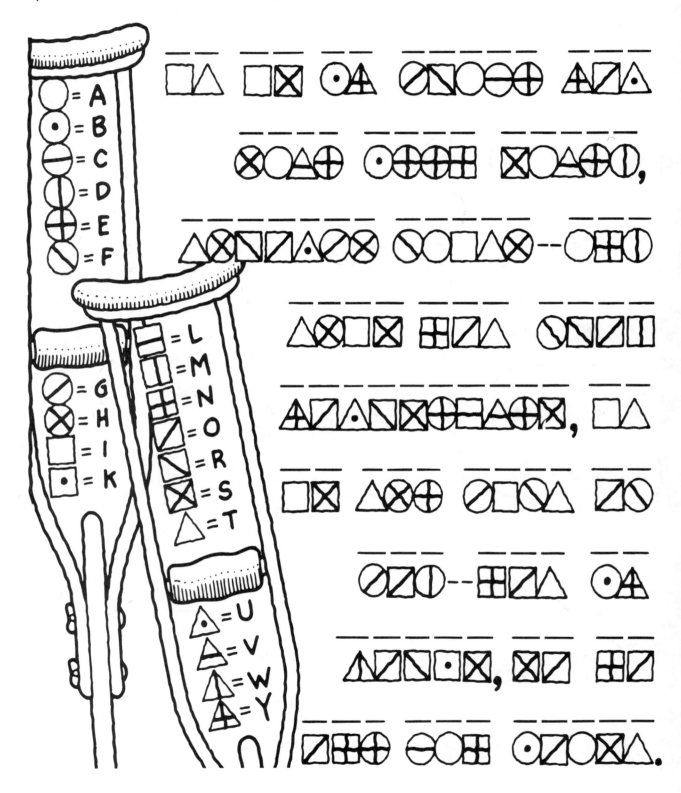

 Through the Bible Puzzles, © 2001 by Standard Publishing • Permission granted to photocopy for classroom use only.

You Can Take It

Read Ephesians 6:10-18 and fill in the blanks below. Using the first or last letter of the word in the blank, follow the lines and write one letter in the box. When you're finished, you'll find a word used four times in Ephesians 6 to describe what believers can do against the devil.

Put _____ the full armor of God.

Our struggle is against the _____ forces of evil.

Put on the _____ of truth.

The shield of faith will extinguish the _____ of the evil one.

The sword of the Spirit is the _____ of God.

Through the Bible Puzzles, © 2001 by Standard Publishing • Permission granted to photocopy for classroom use only.

What Should You Think?

Read Philippians 4:4-9 and Colossians 1:9-14. Find your way through the brain maze by "picking up" words that should fill your thoughts.

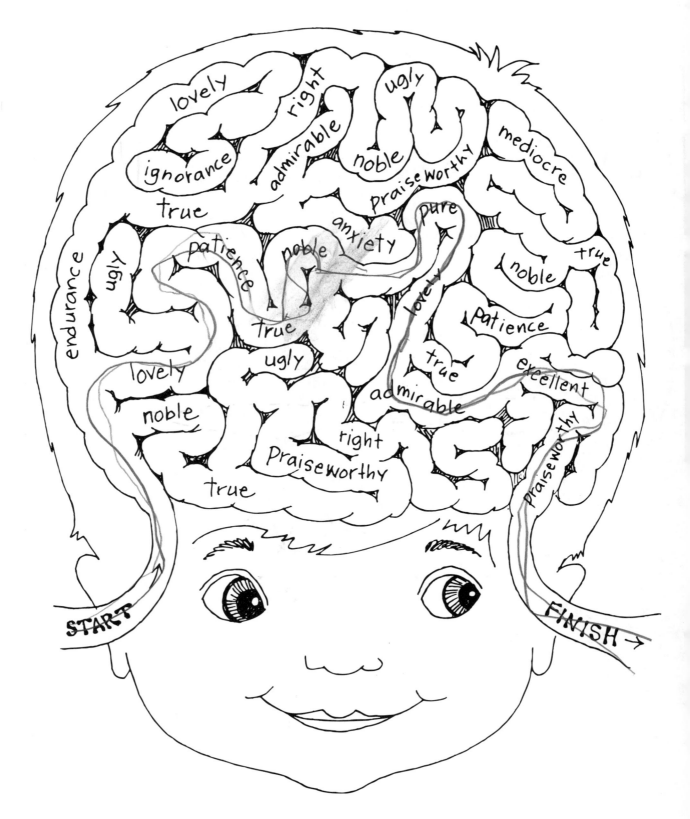

Through the Bible Puzzles, © 2001 by Standard Publishing • Permission granted to photocopy for classroom use only.

Not to Fear

Read 1 Thessalonians 4:13-18 and Revelation 22:6, 7. Start with box A. Put the first letter of the object in that box on the line provided. Then do the same with boxes B, C, D, and so on.

Whether we fall asleep in the Lord, or are caught up with him in the clouds, there's nothing to fear.

_____

_____

Through the Bible Puzzles, © 2001 by Standard Publishing • Permission granted to photocopy for classroom use only.

Fight the Good Fight

Read 1 Timothy 1:18, 19; 4:7-12. Paul gives Timothy some good advice. For each line of letters, first write in order all the uppercase letters. Then write in order on the second line all the lowercase letters.

Paul told Timothy to hold on to

goFodcAoulTscienHce

_____

_____

Paul told Timothy to set an example in

SiPEifEeCH

_____

_____

fLOaiVtEh

_____

_____

ApNuriDty

_____

_____

 Through the Bible Puzzles, © 2001 by Standard Publishing • Permission granted to photocopy for classroom use only.

What Is Faith?

Read Hebrews 11:1-6. Decode the quiz by changing the letters as indicated in the code box.

From	C	N	W	P	S	D	L	I	A	O	T	F	U	E	R	H	B
To	A	B	C	D	E	F	G	H	I	N	O	P	R	S	T	U	W

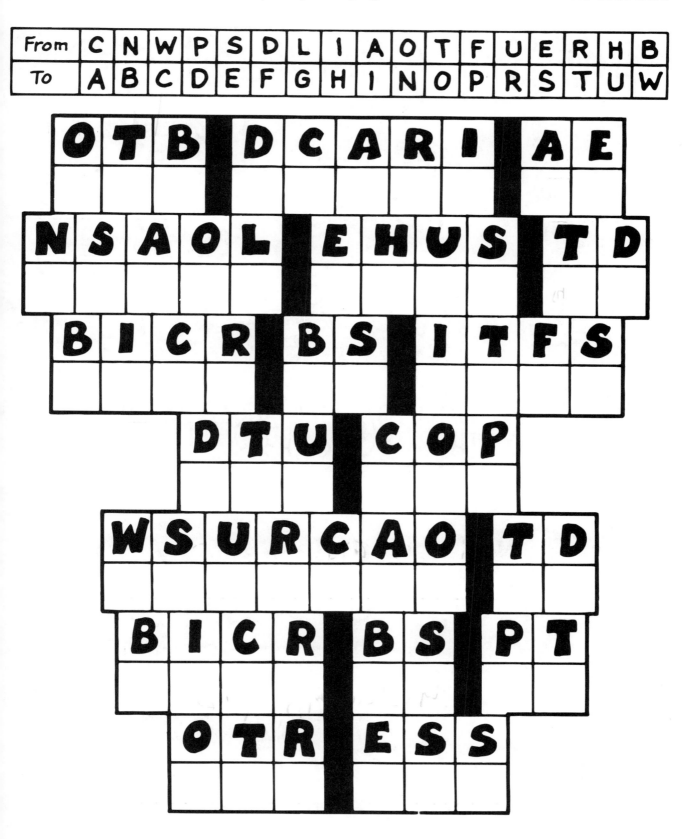

Active Faith

Read James 2:14-26. Find the message by writing the words in the matching shapes.

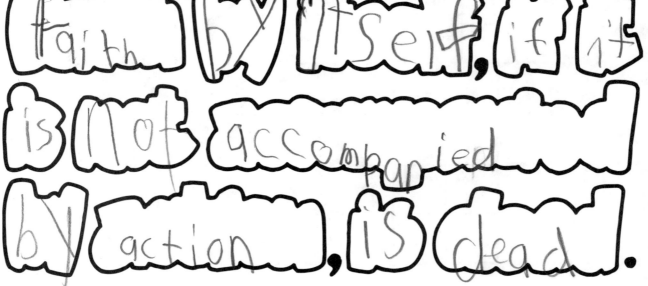

Faith by itself, if it is not accompanied by action, is dead.

 Through the Bible Puzzles, © 2001 by Standard Publishing • Permission granted to photocopy for classroom use only.

Show Love

ead 1 John 4:7-12, 19-21. To fill in the boxes, begin at one of the lettered boxes. Follow the
e that leads from it to another empty box and put that letter in the empty box.

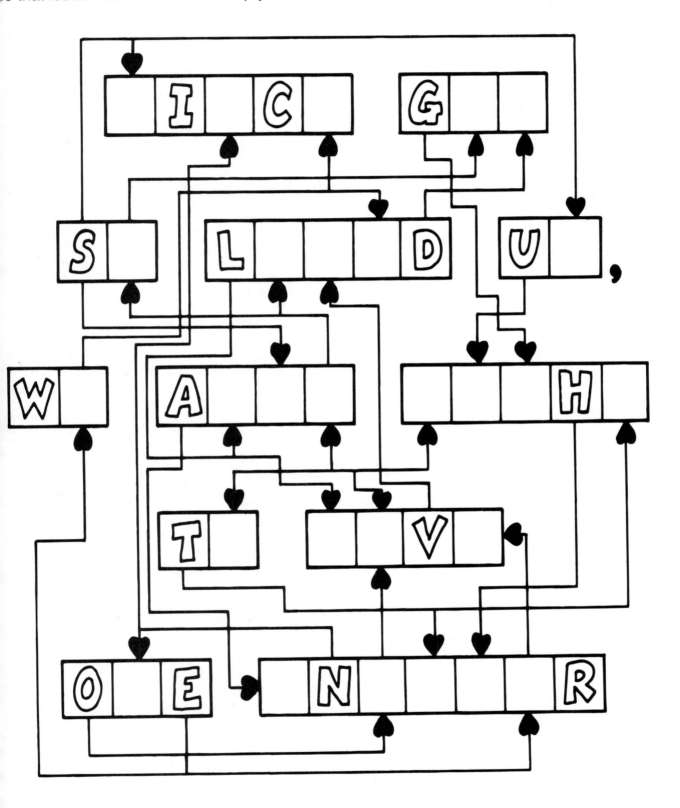

Through the Bible Puzzles, © 2001 by Standard Publishing • Permission granted to photocopy for classroom use only.

Answers

Let There Be, p. 6
Day 1 (picture 4, light/dark), Day 2 (picture 5, water/sky), Day 3 (picture 2, trees/plants), Day 4 (picture 3, sun/moon/stars), Day 5 (picture 1, sea creatures/birds), Day 6 (picture 6, animals)

The Beginning, p. 7
God created all things with his almighty power.

Something Special, p. 8
God created man in his own image.

Strange Tree, p. 9
The first sin came into the world when Adam and Eve disobeyed God and ate of the tree of the knowledge of good and evil.

Where Are You?, p. 10
Why did Adam and Eve try to hide from God?

Offerings, p. 11
Abel's offering came from his heart.

Rainbows, p. 12
Never again will all life be cut off by the waters of a flood.

The Promise, p. 13
I will make you into a great nation and I will bless you.

Separation, p. 14
If you go to the left, I'll go to the right; if you go to the right, I'll go to the left.

Who's Who?, p. 15
1-Abraham, 2-three men, 3-Sarah, 4-servant, 5-the Lord, 6-child; promise

A Lot to Learn, p. 16
1-Sodom, 2-Lot, 3-destroy, 4-wife, 5-sulfur, 6-pillar, 7-rising; Sin brings punishment.

Stop!, p. 17
"Do not lay a hand on the boy," he said. "Do not do anything to him. Now I know that you fear God, because you have not withheld from me your son, your only son."

Family Ties, p. 18
Here is Rebekah; take her and go, and let her become the wife of your master's son, as the Lord has directed.

Brothers, p. 19
Esau sold his birthright to Jacob.

Heavenly Ladder, p. 20
This is none other than the house of God; this is the gate of heaven.

Children of Israel, p. 21
Reuben, Benjamin, Naphtali, Issachar, Joseph, Dan, Simeon, Judah, Levi, Gad, Asher, Zebulun.

Oh Brother!, p. 22
Israel, dream, flocks, Reuben, robe, cistern, Midianite, Egypt; DREAMER

Who's in Charge?, p. 23
Pharaoh said to Joseph, "Since God has made all this known to you, . . . I hereby put you in charge of the whole land of Egypt."

Food for Thought, p. 24
A-4, fish; B-2, banana; C-3, tomato; C-1, pickle; B-4, onion; D-2, steak; famine.

Family Reunion, p. 25
Three Os diagonally (top left to bottom right)

Egyptian Inscription, p. 26
Reuben, Simeon, Levi, Judah, Issachar, Zebulun, Benjamin, Dan, Naphtali, Gad, Asher

Baby in a Basket, p. 27
When the child grew older, she took him to Pharaoh's daughter and he became her son. She named him Moses, saying, "I drew him out of the water."

Scrambled Plagues, p, 28
Boils, darkness, flies, waters to blood, gnats, livestock die, hail, locusts; Let the Israelites go.

Eat and Run, p. 29
Passover

Our Passover Lamb, p. 30
1-T, 2-F, 3-T, 4-T, 5-T, 6-F, 7-T, 8-T, 9-T, 10-T, 11-T; Jesus Christ

Walls of Water, p. 31
That day the Lord saved Israel from the hands of the Egyptians.

Food for Thought, p. 32
At twilight you will eat meat, and in the morning you will be filled with bread. Then you will know that I am the Lord your God. Exodus 16:12

The Ten Commandments, p. 33
1-gods, 2-idols, 3-name, 4-Sabbath, 5-Honor, 6-murder, 7-adultery, 8-steal, 9-false, 10-covet.

Beware of Imitations, p. 34
You shall have no other gods before me.

Respect, p. 35
You shall not misuse the name of the Lord your God. Exodus 20:7

Ring the Bells, p. 36
Remember the Sabbath day by keeping it holy.

The Promise, p. 37
Honor your father and your mother, so that you may live long in the land the Lord your God is giving you.

Honesty, p. 38
You shall not give false testimony against your neighbor.

Leave It Alone, p. 39
You shall not covet your neighbor's house. You shall not covet anything that belongs to your neighbor.

The Tabernacle, p. 40
Have them make a sanctuary for me and I will dwell among them.

Written in Stone, p. 41
The tablets were the work of God; the writing was the writing of God engraved on the tablets.

In Numbers, p. 42
Canaan, tribe, forty, milk, honey, stronger, Joshua, pleased, lead

Thirst Aid, p. 43

Then Moses raised his arm and struck the rock twice with his staff. Water gushed out, and the community and their livestock drank.

But Why, Lord?, p. 44

Follow God's law for a happy life.

Do It Right, p. 45

Love the Lord your God with all your heart and with all your soul and with all your strength. Deuteronomy 6:5

Welcome Home, p. 46

No. Yes. Yes. No. No; They crossed on dry ground.

Shout!, p. 47

Joshua, Jericho, trumpets, seven, shouted, collapsed

Achan's Sin, p. 48

You can not hide your sins from God.

Remember the Promise, p.49

1-Your forefathers . . . lived beyond the river. 2-I led Abraham throughout Canaan. 3-To Abraham I gave Isaac. 4-To Isaac I gave Jacob and Esau. 5-Jacob and his sons went down to Egypt. 6-I sent Moses and Aaron and brought you out of Egypt. 7-You lived in the desert for a long time. 8-I gave you a land on which you did not toil. Now serve God with all faithfulness.

Lead the Way, p. 50

1-True, 2-True, 3-False, 4-True, 5-True, 6-True, 7-True, 8-False, 9-False. The Israelites defeated Sisera's army with the Lord's help.

Surprise!, p. 51

They shouted, "A sword for the Lord and for Gideon!"

Samson's Weakness, p. 52

1-Samson, 2-slaves, 3-love, 4-Delilah, 5-secret, 6-strength, 7-razor, 8-shaved, 9-hair, 10-asleep, 11-lost, 12-prison, 13-perform, 14-prayed, 15-pillars, 16-temple

What a Friend!, p. 53

She was loyal to Naomi.

Here I Am!, p. 54

Speak, for your servant is listening.

Sounds Like, p. 55

1-ring/king, 2-live/give, 3-can/man, 4-reader/leader, 5-soil/oil, 6-steeple/people

Look Inside, p. 56

The Lord chose David son of Jesse to be king over Israel.

Stones, 'n Stuff, p. 57

1-shepherd's bag, 2-Philistine, 3-boy, 4-sword, spear, javelin, 5-Lord Almighty, 6-know, 7-forehead, 8-killed. The whole world will know that there is a God in Israel.

Friends Forever, p, 58

1-kill, 2-warned, 3-loved, 4-friendship, 5-son

Have Mercy on Me!, p. 59

(1) May the Lord judge between (2) you and me. And may (3) the Lord avenge the wrongs (4) you have done to me, (5) but my hand will not (6) touch you.

The Wise King, p. 60

1-Solomon, 2-heart, 3-pleased, 4-riches, honor, long life

Good Advice, p. 61

Give them a favorable answer. Tell them you will make their yoke even heavier.

Help From on High, p. 62

Bread, water, meat

Rescue Recipe, p. 63

Handful of flour in a jar. Little oil in a jug.

And the Winner Is, p. 64

The fire of the Lord fell and burned up the sacrifice.

Whirlwind Words, p. 65

Elijah, whirlwind, Lord, Jericho, prophets, Jordan, Elisha, cloak, fire, heaven

What a Blessing!, p. 66

1-meal, 2-chair, 3-son, 4-noon, 5-house, 6-eyes, 7-sneezed, 8-call, 9-feet

Who Said That?, p. 67

1-Naaman, 2-young girl, 3-King of Aram, 4-Elisha, 5-King of Israel; "If only my master . . ."(young girl), "Am I God?" (King of Israel), "Go, Wash yourself . . ." (Elisha), "Are not Abana . . ." (Naaman), "By all means, go." (King of Aram)

Bad Shape, p. 68

They sinned and worshiped other gods.

What Was Their Downfall?, p. 69

1-sinned, 2-practices, 3-high, 4-stones, 5-wicked, 6-idols, 7-stiff-necked, 8-rejected, 9-worthless, 10-anger

Our God Is Greater, p. 70

Build, temple, Name, great, Moriah, praise, forever, "He is good; his love endures forever."

Work Boxes, p.71

Brought their money gladly.

The Secret of Success, p. 72

As long as he sought the Lord, God gave him success.

Construction Site, p. 73

It had been done with the help of our God.

A Brave Queen, p. 74

I will go to the king, even though it is against the law. And if I perish, I perish. Esther 4:16.

Why Me?, p. 75

You can do all things.

Lost Sheep, p. 76

1-pastures, 2-shadow, 3-green, 4-soul, 5-oil, 6-waters, 7-goodness. THE LORD.

Wise Up!, p. 77

1-T, 2-T, 3-T, 4-F, 5-T, 6-T, 7-T, 8-F, 9-T, 10-T, 11-T, 12-T

When the Lord Calls, p. 78

Here I am. Send me.

His Name Is, p, 79

1-Wonderful Counselor, 2-Mighty God, 3-Everlasting Father, 4-Prince of Peace, 5-Son of the Most High, 6-Son of God

Missing Alphabet, p. 80

God has no equal!

The Prophet, p. 81

Isaiah

Taking Shape, p. 82

1-artist, 2-frame, 3-hook, 4. pen, 5-you'd, 6-lily, 7-honey, 8head, 9-tent, 10-china; Like clay in the hand of the potter, so are you in my hand.

Cistern Escape, p. 83

1-army, 2-cistern, 3-courtyard, 4-prophet, 5-dies; ropes

Captured!, p. 84

The captives from Jerusalem and Judah were carried into exile to Babylon.

Follow Directions, p. 85

Zedekiah became king and did evil. He turned away from God. The Babylonian army surrounded the city. People starved. Soon the army broke in and burned everything.

The Lord's Promise, p. 86

I will put my Spirit in you and move you to follow my decrees and be careful to keep my laws, Ezekiel 36 verse 27.

What's on the Menu?, p. 87

Daniel, Shadrach, Meshach, and Abednego, ate vegetables and water. The king's court ate royal food and wine.

God Protects His Faithful, p. 88

Shadrach, Meshach, and Abednego ate were not burned in the furnace because they were true to God.

The King Learns a Lesson, p. 89

1-T, 2-T, 3-F, 4-T, 5-T, 6-F, 7-T, 8-F, 9-T, 10-F; Only God is all powerful.

Handwriting on the Wall, p. 90

The king lost his life, and the message came true because he did not honor God.

Lion Tamer, p, 91

God's angel shut the lions' mouths.

A Straight Wall, p. 92

1-Amos, 2-Uzziah, 3-Israel, 4-Tekoa, 5-years, 6-hand, 7-sanctuaries, 8-Jeroboam, 9-Amaziah, 10-conspiracy, 11-Judah

Crazy Clues, p. 93

1-E, 2-T, 3-O, 4-H, 5-A, 6-Y. They came and began to work on the house of the Lord Almighty.

Give and Receive, p. 94

Bring tithes and offerings to God and you will be blessed.

The Genealogy of Jesus, p. 95

Abraham/Isaac; Isaac/Jacob; Jacob/Judah; Salmon/Boaz; Boaz/Obed; Obed/Jesse; Jesse/David; King David/Solomon. There were 42 generations from Abraham to Christ.

A Gift for Me?, p. 96

Jesus, because he will save his people from their sins.

Come and Worship!, p. 97

1-bowed, 2-east, 3-star, 4-Christ, 5-gold, 6-Jesus, 7-Herod, 8-Judea, 9-Magi; Bethlehem

Star Search, p. 98

Worshiped him!

Jesus Is Baptized, p. 99

The Spirit of God descended like a dove on him.

The Spirit, p. 100

This is my Son, whom I love; with him I am well pleased.

Yield Not to Temptation, p. 101

Worship the Lord your God.

Calling Followers, p. 102

Peter, James, John, Andrew, Judas, Bartholomew, Matthew, Thomas, James, Simon, Thaddaeus, Philip; Apostles.

Who Is Blessed?, p. 103

Mountain

What Am I?, p. 104

You are the salt of the earth. You are the light of the world. A city on a hill cannot be hidden. But if the salt loses its saltiness, how can it be made salty again?

A Wise Builder, p. 105

A wise builder is one who hears these words and puts them into practice.

Twelve Men, p. 106

1-Andrew, 2-Simon, 3-Thomas, 4-Judas Iscariot, 5-Simon Peter, 6-Philip, 7-Bartholomew, 8-James, 9-Thaddaeus. The other three are James son of Zebedee, John, and Matthew.

Find the Treasure, p. 107

1-treasure, 2-field, 3-man, 4-joy, 5-merchant, 6-pearls, 7-value

Cross It Out, p. 108

You shall not commit adultery. Herod wanted to kill John.

Jesus Walked on Water, p. 109

Then those who were in the boat worshiped him, saying, "Truly you are the Son of God."

Peter's Confession Hourglass, p. 110

1-disciples, 2-Philippi, 3-blessed, 4-region, 5-Jonah, 6-some, 7-who, 8-do, 9-is, 10-you, 11-John, 12-Jesus, 13-Jeremiah, 16-living God

Forgive, p. 111

I tell you, not seven times, but seventy-seven times.

Two Sons, p. 112

Two, first, son, work, vineyard, will not, son, should, father, son, work, vineyard, yes, will, two, first. Change and believe. Enter the kingdom.

When Will Jesus Come?, p. 113

Keep watch, because you do not know the day or the hour.

One Talent, p. 114

Hid it in the ground.

What's the Question?, p. 115

Sheep or goat?

See the Stone?, p. 116

The women went to the tomb and found the stone rolled back. An angel told them, "Jesus is risen."

A Final Message, p. 117

Jesus said, "Go and make disciples of all nations, baptizing them in the name of the Father and of the Son and of the Holy Spirit, and teaching them to obey everything I have commanded you."

Forgiven!, p. 118

Son, your sins are forgiven. That you may know that the Son of Man has authority on earth to forgive sins.

Healing of the Demon-Possessed Man, p. 119

1-T, 2-F, 3-F, 4-T, 5-T, 6-F, 7-T, 8-T

A Rich Man's Mistake, p. 120
He went away sad because he had great wealth.

A Slave, p. 121
Whoever wants to be first must be slave of all.

Important Phone Call, p. 122
Love the Lord your God with all your heart. Love your neighbor as yourself.

The Widow's Offering, p. 123
Everything

Missing Word ABCs, p. 124
Alexander, Bottom, Curtain, Darkness, Elijah, Forsaken, Golgotha, Heard, In, Jews, King, Lots, Myrrh, Ninth, Offered, Passing, Robbers, Sponge, Third, Until

Alleluia!, p. 125
1-Arimathea, 2-Pilate, 3-body, 4-wrapped, 5-in, 6-stone, 7-entrance, 8-spices, 9-Jesus, 10-man, 11-robe, 12-right, 13-alarmed. The Lord is risen. Be glad.

Chrono-Code, p. 126
Your prayer has been heard.

The News, p. 127
Child, birth, son, Jesus, Lord's servant, said

It's a Boy!, p. 128
His name is John.

A Savior, p. 129
Today in the town of David a Savior has been born to you; he is Christ the Lord.

Scrambled Rulers, p. 130
Quirinius, Caesar, David, Augustus, Governor, Christ, Lord. Today a Savior has been born!

Jumble John, p. 131
Tax collectors, soldiers, people, crowd, God, Annas, Caiaphas, Zechariah. Good News.

Fishers of Men, p. 132
1-edge, 2-washing, 3-Simon, 4-catch, 5-night, 6-partners, 7-fell, 8-Zebedee, 9-Jesus; disciples

The Alabaster Jar, p. 133
Forgiven

Good Soil, p. 134
Seed, good, soil, noble, good, heart, word, persevering, produce, crop

Jesus Calms a Stormy Sea, p. 135
He commands even the winds and the water, and they obey him.

Just Believe, p. 136
"My child, get up!" Her spirit returned.

The Glory of the Lord, p. 137
1-eight, 2-John, 3-pray, 4-face, 5-clothes, 6-Two, 7-very, 8-cloud, 9-cloud, 10-listen to, 11-no one

A Good Neighbor, p. 138
1-b, 2-c, 3-a, 4-c

What Did Martha Open?, p. 139
1-The Lord's, 2-upset, 3-listened, 4-hearing, 5-teach, 6-Mary; her home.

Decode the Prayer, p. 140
Ask and it will be given to you; seek and you will find; knock and the door will be opened to you.

Rich Man, p. 141
Fool, night, life, demanded, who, get, prepared, yourself, stores, himself, rich, toward, God

Repent!, p. 142
Sink, nut, ear, rake, pen, toes, rain, ghost, one, house. Sinner, repents, righteous.

Lost and Found, p. 143
1-cane, 2-lace, 3-bear, 4-ant, 5-end, 6-apron, 7-dew, 8-ants, 9-gull, 10-add. Celebrated and was glad.

The Rich Man and Lazarus, p. 144
Abraham, Lazarus, five, purple, listen, luxury, sores, convinced, torment. Have pity on me.

Amazingly Healed, p. 145
1-Jerusalem, 2-ten men, 3-Jesus, Master, 4-cleansed, 5-praising, 6-Samaritan, 7-ten, 8-well

The Pharisee and the Tax Collector, p. 146
God, have mercy on me, a sinner. God, I thank you that I am not like this tax collector.

A Short Story, p. 147
Sycamore, Zacchaeus, cheated, tax collector, come down, four times, stay, Jericho, salvation. You shall not steal.

Praise God!, p. 148
Blessed is the king who comes in the name of the Lord! Peace in heaven and glory in the highest!

Amazing Love, p. 149
For God so loved the world that he gave his one and only Son that whoever believes in him shall not perish but have eternal life.

Worship, p. 150
God is spirit and his worshipers must worship in spirit and in truth.

One Lunch That Fed More Than 5,000, p. 151
How far will they go among so many? They had enough to eat. Twelve baskets of barley loaves were left over.

Lazarus, Come Out!, p. 152
Many of the Jews put their faith in him.

Jesus Is Risen, p. 153
Puzzle 1: 3; Puzzle 2: 5; Puzzle 3: 2; He is not here; he has risen.

Easter Morning, p. 154
1-F, 2-T, 3-T, 4-F, 5-T, 6-F, 7-T, 8-F, 9-T, 10-F; Jesus arose!

Miraculous Catch of Fish, p. 155
Across: 1-I'm, 3-with, 4-raised, 6-answered, 7-disciples
Down: 2-him, 3-water, 5-dragged, 6-afterward

Seek the Truth, p. 156
1-T, 2-F, 3-T, 4-F, 5-F, 6-T; Receive the power of the Spirit.

Cross It Out, p. 157
1-wind, fire, sound, tongues, 2-Peter, 3-Pentecost, 4-Jerusalem, 5-repent, be baptized, save yourselves, 6-3,000, 7-Israel, 8-eleven, apostles, 9-heard, accepted, were baptized, 10-Jews. God made Jesus both Lord and Christ

Finding Words, p. 158
Breaking, teaching, selling, being, everything, enjoying, praising; believers.

What Did the People Think?, p. 159
1-Peter, John; 2-pray; 3-beautiful; 4-something; 5-gold; 6-Nazareth; 7-jumped, walk; They were filled with wonder and amazement at what had happened to him.

On Trial, p. 160

Peter and John were arrested for talking about Jesus. Peter said the people had crucified Jesus. The rulers were astonished at the courage Peter and John showed but warned them not to speak of Jesus.

What's in a Name?, p. 161

1-believers, 2-shared, 3-great, 4-testify, 5-resurrection, 6-needy, 7-lands, houses, 8-money; Son of encouragement

Stephen's Last Stand, p. 162

Blue: God's grace, power, wonders, miraculous, wisdom, Holy Spirit, Heaven, Jesus
Red: opposition, argue, furious, gnashed, yelling, rushed, dragged, stone

The Ethiopian's Question, p. 163

Look, here is water. Why shouldn't I be baptized?

Saul's Conversion, p. 164

Persecutor, believer, light, blinded, Ananias, sight, called, witness, baptized, Christian

Joy in Joppa, p. 165

1-Joppa, 2-Tabitha, 3-Dorcas, 4-Lydda, 5-Peter, 6-disciples, 7-men, 8-widows, 9-believers, 10-people; Many people believed in the Lord.

Right or Wrong?, p. 166

Peter learned not to call any man impure or unclean.

Christians Scatter, p. 167

Stephen, Barnabas, Antioch, Christians, disciples

Good News!, p. 168

1-Saul, 2-fasted, 3-speak, 4-Jesus, 5-death. Peach-cabbage-cabbage-kiwi. Lettuce-grapefruit-zucchini-corn; Good News

Paul and Barnabas, p. 169

The Lord used the early Christians to perform miracles. We are bringing you good news, telling you to turn from these worthless things to the living God.

Prison, p. 170

The jailer and his family were saved.

The Unknown God, p. 171

1-from the dead, 2-world, 3-Heaven, earth, 4-nation, man; 5-have our being

Spreading the Word, p. 172

Frauds, beat them. The word of the Lord spread widely and grew in power.

Paul's Mission, p. 173

Miletus, elders, humility, Holy Spirit, Jews, Greeks, prison, God, nothing, shepherds, watch, tears; Tell the Good News.

Shipwreck, p. 174

Keep up your courage, not one of you will be lost.

Love, Love, Love, p. 175

Share with God's people who are in need. Love must be sincere. Be joyful in hope. Be careful to do what is right. Live in harmony. Practice hospitality.

The Lord's Supper, p. 176

Do this in remembrance of me.

Mixed Fruit, p. 177

Love, joy, peace, patience, kindness, goodness, faith fulness, gentleness, self-control

Helpful Crutches, p. 178

It is by grace you have been saved, through faith—and this not from yourselves, it is the gift of God, not by works, so no one can boast.

You Can Take It, p. 179

Put on the belt of truth. Our struggle is against the spiritual forces of evil. Put on the full armor of God. The shield of faith will extinguish the arrows of the evil one. The sword of the spirit is the word of God. Stand.

What Should You Think?, p. 180

Lovely, patience, true, noble, pure, lovely, admirable, excellent, praiseworthy

Not to Fear, p. 181

We will be with the Lord forever.

Fight the Good Fight, p. 182

Faith, good conscience, speech, life, love, faith, and purity

What Is Faith?, p. 183

Now faith is being sure of what we hope for and certain of what we do not see.

Active Faith, p. 184

Faith by itself, if it is not accompanied by action, is dead.

Show Love, p. 185

Since God so loved us, we also ought to love one another.

Standard Publishing Middler Curriculum Syllabus

These two pages list the lesson titles from Standard Publishing's Sunday school curriculum for Middlers (grades 3 and 4). Beside the lesson title is the page number of puzzle(s) in this book that correlate to the lesson. Use the puzzles for early arrivers, early finishers, for rewards, review, or to send to those who missed class.

Autumn, Year One

1. God Is Special (Psalm 66; Romans 11)
2. God Made It All (Genesis 1, 2); pages 7, 8, 9
3. Live God's Way (Genesis 2, 3); pages 10, 11
4. Believe God's Way (Genesis 6–8)
5. Trust God's Way (Genesis 12); page14
6. A Feuding Family (Genesis 37); pages 23, 24, 25
7. Servant's Heart (Genesis 41); page 25
8. Forgiving Spirit (Genesis 42, 45, 47); page 26
9. God Cares for Moses (Exodus 2, 3); page 28
10. God Uses Moses (Exodus 7); page 29
11. God Cares for the Israelites (Exodus 11, 12); pages 30, 31
12. God Protects the Israelites (Exodus 12, 14); page 32
13. God Guides the Israelites (Exodus 19, 20); pages 34-46

Winter, Year One

1. A New Leader (Deuteronomy 34; Joshua 1); page 48
2. A New Home (Joshua 3); page 47
3. A New Family (Matthew 1); pages 96, 127-130
4. A New Start (Joshua 6); page 48
5. A Son Is Born (Ruth 1, 2, 4); page 49
6. A Shepherd Is King (Psalm 23); pages 58, 77
7. A King Is Wise (2 Chronicles 1; Proverbs 3)
8. The Crumbled Kingdom (1 Kings 12); page 61
9. The Repaired Temple (2 Chronicles 24); page 71
10. The Pottery Lesson (Jeremiah 18); page 82
11. Wise Choice (Daniel 1); page 87
12. Courageous Choice (Daniel 6); page 91
13. Best Choice (Jeremiah 29; 2 Chronicles 36; Ezra 1)

Spring, Year One

1. How Can I Be Sure? (Luke 1); pages 126-128
2. How Can I Grow? (Luke 2); pages 129, 130
3. How Can I Get Ready? (Luke 3); page 131
4. How Can I Serve? (Matthew 4, 10); pages 101,102
5. Jesus' Power to Overcome Evil (Mark 5); page 119
6. Jesus' Power to Heal (Matthew 8)
7. Jesus' Power to Give Sight (Mark 10)
8. Jesus' Power to Overcome Death (Matthew 27; John 19); pages 116, 153
9. Have Mercy! (Matthew 18); page 111
10. Use It or Lose It (Matthew 25); page 114
11. Watch It Grow (Luke 8); page 134
12. Help! I'm Lost! (Luke 15); page 143
13. Follow the Blueprint (Matthew 7); page 105

Summer, Year One

1. Let Us Pray (Matthew 6)
2. Don't Give Up (Luke 11); page 140
3. Peter Preaches (Acts 2); pages 157, 158
4. Peter Heals (Acts 3); page 159
5. Peter Witnesses (Acts 4); page 160, 161
6. Peter Raises the Dead (Acts 9); page 165
7. Peter Learns (Acts 10); page 166
8. Peter Escapes (Acts 12)
9. Be Strong! (Ephesians 6); page 179
10. Be Good! (Romans 12); page 175
11. Be Fruitful! (Galatians 5); page 177
12. Be Loving! (1 John 4); page 185
13. Be Joyful! (Revelation 1, 7, 15)

Standard Publishing Middler Curriculum Syllabus

Autumn, Year Two
1. The Bible Is God's Word (Deuteronomy 8; Psalm 119)
2. The Earth Is God's Work (Genesis 1; Psalm 104); pages 6, 7
3. The Tower Is Man's Rebellion (Genesis 11)
4. A Promise (Genesis 17, 18, 21); page 15
5. A Test (Genesis 22); page 17
6. A Struggle (Genesis 25); page 19
7. A Prophetess of Honor (Judges 4, 5); page 50
8. A Mighty Warrior (Judges 6, 7); pages 47, 48
9. A Reluctant King (1 Samuel 8–10); page 55
10. A Faithful Servant (1 Samuel 12)
11. A Foolish King (1 Kings 12–14); pages 61
12. An Obedient Prophet (1 Kings 17); pages 62, 63
13. A Grateful Mother (2 Kings 4); page 66

Winter, Year Two
1. A Prophet Obeys (Jonah 1, 3)
2. A Queen Is Brave (Esther); page 74
3. A Ruler Is Coming (Isaiah 7, 9, 40); page 79
4. Jesus Is Born (Luke 2); pages 129,130
5. Jesus Is Taken to the Temple (Luke 2)
6. Jesus Receives Gifts (Matthew 2); pages 97, 98
7. Jesus Corrects (John 2)
8. Jesus Teaches (John 3); page 149
9. Jesus Heals (Luke 4)
10. Jesus Chose Twelve (Matthew 9; Luke 6; John 1)
11. Jesus Taught Joy (Matthew 5); page 103
12. Jesus Gave Peace (Matthew 8)
13. Jesus Meets Needs (John 6); page 151

Spring, Year Two
1. A Great Confession (Matthew 16); page 110
2. An Amazing Sight (Luke 9); page 137
3. A Miraculous Event (John 11); page 152
4. Guide for Living (Matthew 22)
5. An Important Teaching (Matthew 25); pages 113-115
6. A Special Meal (Mark 14)
7. The Ultimate Miracle (Mark 14–16); page 129
8. Jesus Is Alive! (John 20); page 154
9. A Surprise Visit (Luke 24)
10. Final Instructions (Matthew 28; Acts 1); pages 117, 156
11. A Forgiving Witness (Acts 6, 7); page 162
12. A Teaching Witness (Acts 8); page 163
13. A Changed Witness (Acts 9); page 164

Summer, Year Two
1. Preaching and Teaching (Acts 14); pages 168, 169
2. Saving the Lost (Acts 16)
3. Praising in Prison (Acts 16); page 170
4. Raising the Dead (Acts 20); page 173
5. Plotting to Kill (Acts 23)
6. A Dangerous Journey (Acts 27, 28); page 174
7. Important Instructions (Romans); page 175
8. Live Right (Ephesians 4–6 ; 1 Thessalonians 3–5); page 181
9. Stand Strong (Philippians); page 180
10. Have Faith (Titus 2, 3)
11. Seek Wisdom (James); page 184
12. The Final Judgment (Revelation 5, 11, 12, 14, 15)
13. The Final Triumph! (Revelation 1, 3, 22)